In the Ranks

of the

C.I.V.

IN THE RANKS

OF THE

C.I.V.

BY

ERSKINE CHILDERS

The Spellmount Library of Military History

SPELLMOUNT
Staplehurst

British Library Cataloguing in Publication Data:
A catalogue record for this book is available
from the British Library

Copyright © Spellmount Ltd 1999
Introduction © Ian Knight 1999

ISBN 1-86227-053-8

First published in 1901

This edition first published in the UK in 1999
in
The Spellmount Library of Military History
by
Spellmount Limited
The Old Rectory
Staplehurst
Kent TN12 0AZ

1 3 5 7 9 8 6 4 2

Printed in Great Britain by
T.J.International Ltd
Padstow, Cornwall

AN INTRODUCTION
By Ian Knight

Erskine Childers' *In the Ranks of the C.I.V.* is a remarkable history in a number of respects. For one thing, it is an account of a Victorian military campaign written by a man in the ranks, at a time when such accounts were still a rarity. Although it was something of a literary convention in the late nineteenth century for retired officers in the army and navy to write their memoirs, it was unusual for ordinary soldiers to do so, if only because the steady increase in educational standards within the Victorian army had not yet reached the point at which the average soldier was able to express himself at such length. Not that Childers was an average soldier; rather, he was typical of the middle-class volunteers who flocked to join units such as the C.I.V.s in the patriotic fervour that marked the first months of the Anglo-Boer War. Moreover, his account of his adventures is particularly interesting as the first published work by the man who would later become famous as the author of *The Riddle of the Sands*, one of the most famous and influential novels of the Edwardian era.

If *The Riddle of the Sands*, with its dire warning of the threat posed by the emerging German power in Europe, and the danger of British military unpreparedness, is clearly the product of the same intense patriotism which motivated Childers to volunteer in the C.I.V., then it is all the more remarkable to discover that Childers later came to question the righteousness of the Empire, and became a passionate advocate of Irish Home Rule. This cause led him to risk his impressive literary and political reputation, and ultimately to take up arms for the Republican side in the Irish Civil War. In a twist worthy of his own novel, Erskine Childers, advocate of Empire, ended his life in Dublin before a firing squad of Irish Free State troops.

Childers' background was typical of his age and class. He was born in 1870, the younger son of Robert Childers, an Orientalist and Bhuddist scholar, and Anna Barton. While the Childers were essentially English by background and outlook, the Bartons were very much a product of the Protestant Ascendancy in Ireland. It was through his mother's family that Erskine gained his first impressions of Ireland, and these became more pronounced when the Childers' family were struck by personal tragedy. In 1876 Robert Childers succumbed to tuberculosis. When his wife displayed symptoms of the same disease, she was hurried into a sanatorium, and separated from her children to prevent their infection. Left effectively orphaned, the young Childers were raised by Anna's relatives on their estate of Glendalough, south of Dublin. Nevertheless, when he was old enough, young Erskine returned to England and boarding school, and the remainder of his youth was conventional enough; public school, Cambridge, and a job as a clerk in the House of Commons.

Despite a rather bookish manner and appearance, Childers discovered a fondness for adventure at an early age, and it was during his time in London that he developed a passion for yachting. A sailing trip to Europe in 1897 introduced him to the German Frisian Islands, and sowed the seed for the story which would become *The Riddle of the Sands*.

His plans to write the novel were interrupted, however, by the outbreak of the Anglo-Boer War in 1899. The war began badly, with a series of defeats in December 1899 which shocked the British Empire to its core. At the height of Imperial pomp and circumstance, when huge blocks of the world map were painted British red, it seemed inconceivable that a handful of uncouth farmers could humble famous British generals and cast the name of England in the dust. Volunteers flocked to enlist to fight the Boers, not only at home, but throughout the Empire. The City Imperial Volunteers were raised by the City of London, and their ranks were filled largely by London office-workers. Childers himself was prompted to join by patriotism, by a commitment to the values and principles which the Empire was widely held to champion, and by a personal desire to serve his country.

Childers says little about the origins of Anglo-Boer conflict in his book. In many respects, the war was a clash between two very different forms of imperialism. The Boers were the descendants of the Dutch settlers who established a toe-hold on the southern tip of Africa in the seventeenth century. Over the years, reinforced by a steady trickle of French and German refugees from Europe, and assuming some of the attitudes of the African groups among whom they lived, the Dutch came to think of themselves as a distinct people, *Afrikaners* – white Africans – or more simply, *Boers* – farmers. The Boers were essentially pastoralists, who depended for their subsistence on their livestock and by hunting. By the end of the eighteenth century, Boer society had assumed an expansionist dynamic, creeping out beyond the confines of the old Cape Colony in search of good grazing land. This movement brought them into contact with the robust African societies beyond, and led to more than a century of endemic conflict.

The British had arrived at the Cape early in the nineteenth century, during the shifting political fortunes which characterised the Napoleonic Wars in Europe. Initially, British interests were confined to the Cape, which, until the advent of the Suez Canal commanded the long haul by sea to India. The Boer frontier farmers resented the advent of British authority, however, and blamed the British for failing to protect their farms against African attacks on the turbulent Eastern Cape frontier. In the 1830s, hundreds of Boer families demonstrated their rejection of the British administration by trekking beyond the colonial frontiers, in the hope of establishing independent territories in the African interior.

The Great Trek was marked by a series of conflicts with indigenous African groups, but it re-drew the political map of southern Africa. The Boers established two republics in the interior, the Orange Free State and Transvaal, while the British retained the Cape, and later extended their authority up the eastern coast by the acquisition of Natal. The British were reluctant to abandon their sovereignty over the Boers, and there were several clashes in the 1840s. The Boers nonetheless retained their independence until the 1870s, when the British annexed the Transvaal as part of a broader attempt to bring the whole of southern Africa more tightly under their control. The British plan foundered in the aftermath of the early disasters of the Anglo-Zulu War in 1879, however, and in 1881 republican elements within the Transvaal rose in revolt, inflicting a series of reverses on British troops which culminated in the crushing defeat at Majuba Hill. The British agreed to restore Boer authority, retaining only a vague claim to suzereignty. Neither in these negotiations, nor in the subsequent ones at the end of the Anglo-Boer War, were the rights and claims of the original African inhabitants – who made up by far the majority of the population in the republic – seriously taken into account.

Political rivalry between the republics and the British continued, given an added piquancy by the discovery of gold in the Transvaal in the 1880s. In the gold rush that followed, most of the diggers who flocked to the new boom town of Johannesburg were *uitlanders* – foreigners – many of them British. While the Transvaal government was happy to profit from gold revenues by taxing the miners, it was reluctant to accord them political rights, realising that they would swamp the influence of the Boers themselves. The bitter complaints of the *uitlanders* provoked the British to take up their cause in the name of liberty and freedom.

The 1890s were, in any case, a time of intensified Imperial activity in southern Africa. The discovery of mineral wealth merely intensified the ambition of Imperial visionaries, like Cecil Rhodes, who dreamed of building a corridor of red 'from Cape to Cairo'. The emergence of rival empires in Europe, and in particular Germany's attempt to court the Boer republics as part of her search for 'a place in the sun', had led to the 'scramble for Africa', and a growing hostility among British administrators towards the Boer republics. In 1896, Rhodes, then Prime Minister of the Cape, attempted to orchestrate a miners' coup in Johannesburg, and his lieutenant, Dr Leander Starr Jameson, led his famous raid to support it. But the *uitlanders* did not rise, and Jameson's force was surrounded by the Boers and captured.

Nevertheless, the Raid marked a turning point on the road to war. The Boer republics, believing a clash to be imminent, imported large quantities of arms from Europe, while both the British Colonial Office, and the administration at the Cape, adopted a more aggressive policy. In June 1899 the High Commissioner at the Cape, Alfred Milner, met Paul Kruger, President of the Transvaal Republic, at Bloemfontein in the Free State, to discuss *uitlander* rights. Milner had already decided to force the issue, and rejected Kruger's offers of compromise. British garrisons in South Africa were prepared for war, and the Boer republics presented an ultimatum demanding that British troops be removed from their borders. The ultimatum expired on 11 October 1899.

Boer forces immediately invaded the British colonies, hoping to win a decisive victory before the British could bring superior resources to bear from overseas. After some initial successes, the Boers managed to invest the main British garrison in Natal at Ladysmith, and to besiege Kimberley in the south and Mafikeng in the north. They were unable to over-run the British positions, however, and their advance bogged down. With the arrival of the mobilised British reserves, the British went onto the offensive, but in November and December 1899 suffered a series of reverses at Stormberg, Modder River, Colenso and Magersfontein, as they tried to penetrate the Boer lines. It was the news of these defeats which prompted the upsurge of patriotic fervour, and the raising of volunteer units.

Childers himself joined the C.I.V. artillery battery (Honourable Artillery Company). By the time he arrived in South Africa in February 1900, however, the war had already turned in Britain's favour. On the western front, the British offensives had relieved Kimberley on the 15th, while in Natal General Buller at last relieved Ladysmith on the 28th. Childers' account, from February to October 1900, therefore covers an important stage of the war; the British were winning the conventional war, and the capture of the republics' capitals lay ahead, while the long and destructive guerrilla war was not yet under way.

Childers' account is also particularly interesting since it provides a contrast to the more common accounts of fighting in Natal. The C.I.V. took part in Lord Roberts' advance on the western front, towards the Free State capital of Bloemfontein, and later the Transvaal capital, Pretoria. This was the period, too, when the Boers, freed from the need to defend a conventional front, first began to use highly mobile columns to attack British supply lines. Childers himself describes some of the events of the British attempts to trap De Wet in the Brandwater basin, against the BaSotholand mountains, the campaign which arguably marked the start of the guerrilla war.

Not that Childers' was privy to the view of the war from the top. On the contrary, the appeal of his book lies in its insights into the way the war appeared to the ordinary soldier in the field. Ill-informed, a prey to every type of rumour, the average British soldier did not concern himself with the grand picture, but was preoccupied instead with his every-day duties, with eating, sleeping, and surviving in a hostile environment. Childers did not take part in the more famous battles of the war, but he did see action, and his description of it paints a vivid picture of the type of fighting which characterised the war, of engagements spread out over many miles, of attacking or defending specific objectives without any clear picture of their tactical significance, of seldom glimpsing an enemy, and of danger heralded by the distant crackle of rifle-fire and the sudden whine and plump of shells landing nearby.

Indeed, it is in the everyday details that Childers' book comes alive; his description of life on the troop-ship, of daily routine, of the difficulties and exhilaration of life in the field, of the cold nights and subtle beauties of the South African highveld dawn, and of the grumblings of the soldiers, who soon came to realise that they were fighting a new type of war, and one for which their enemy was far better prepared than they.

By November of 1900 Childers was back home, invalided out by an infected foot. Like many British troops, he had come to respect the Boers, and was mystified by the hatred felt towards them by English-speaking settlers. While he never questioned the righteousness of the British cause, it is possible that his conversations with Boer prisoners first led him to ponder the fundamental dichotomy between his love of freedom and the nature of empire. Like most British soldiers, however, he did not for a moment pause to extend such consideration to the African community among whom the war was waged.

Most British soldiers believed the war was over by early 1900. In fact, it was entering a new and painful phase, in which Boer commandos traversed the veld almost at will, attacking British columns and supply dumps. Hampered by cumbersome supply trains, the British columns could not match the Boers for speed, and the war degenerated instead into one of attrition. The British struck at the basis of Boer support, destroying farms and herding civilian non-combatants into refugee camps. The later stages of the war created a legacy of bitterness which has not fully healed a century later. The Boers were finally exhausted into submission in May 1902. Altogether, some 8000 British troops had been killed in action, while 13000 more died of disease. Some 4000 Boers were killed, while thousands of women and children died in the cramped conditions in the camps.

Childers published *In The Ranks of the C.I.V.* in 1901, while the war was still in progress. It was a modest commercial success, and prompted a commission to write a history of the H.A.C., and to edit a volume in Leo Amery's *The Times History of the South African War*. These literary successes were soon overshadowed, however, by the publication in May 1903 of his long-awaited novel, *The Riddle of the Sands*.

The Riddle of the Sands concerned the adventures of two friends on a yachting holiday, who stumble across a German plan to invade Britain from the Frisian islands. Although the story has an enduring appeal, Childers had a very specific aim. He was worried by the threat posed by the emergence of Imperial Germany, and he wanted to sound a warning at the dangers of ignoring it. The book was both immediately popular, and successful in its main aim, in that it stimulated a remarkable degree of interest in official circles.

As a result, Childers seemed destined to follow a successful establishment career. In October 1903, however, a chance meeting took his life in a different direction. The H.A.C. had been invited to visit Boston – the first time a British unit had visited America since the Revolution – and it was here that Childers met Molly Osgood, who would become his wife. The Osgoods were staunch republicans, who had many contacts with the Irish republican movement, and it was through them that Childers' interest in Irish affairs was stimulated.

In the first decade of the twentieth century, the Irish issue was a prominent one, for it seemed that the British were at last prepared to relinquish centuries of control, and award a degree of Home Rule. The situation was complicated, however, by the refusal of the predominantly Protestant north – Ulster – to break with the Crown in favour of the Catholic south. The dilemma Irish independence posed to high-minded liberals like Childers was not as pronounced as it now seems, for, like most of his generation, Childers believed the British Empire to be the ultimate expression of Christian liberty and virtue. Thus

Childers' growing passion for the cause of liberty could both cause him to fight for the Empire in South Africa, since he did not doubt the justice of the British cause, and still champion Irish freedom. For Childers, the Irish question became the ultimate test of his very British ideals.

At first, Childers' involvement with Irish issues followed constitutional means. By 1914, however, when it seemed that the split with Ulster threatened to provoke civil war and wreck all progress on Home Rule, he was prepared to put his yachting experience to good use to ship guns from Irish sympathisers in America to republican volunteers. Nevertheless, when the First World War broke out, echoing Childers' fears of the German threat, he immediately volunteered for British service, believing that the war was being waged to prevent German oppression in Europe. Typically, he had an adventurous war, serving with the Royal Naval Air Service in the North Sea – where the knowledge he had drawn upon to write *The Riddle of the Sands* was put to good use – and later in the operations around Gallipoli.

In Easter 1916, however, the republican movement in Ireland orchestrated a rising in Dublin, which was bloodily suppressed. The incident galvanised Childers, who became increasingly disillusioned with British methods, and who began to abandon his commitment towards peaceful change in favour of armed struggle. Once the war was over, Childers and his wife moved to Ireland to immerse themselves in the politics of the struggle. Against a background of accelerating violence – Michael Collins' war against British authority, British reprisals, and the exploits of the Black and Tans – Childers became a staunch supporter of Sinn Fein. With his literary connections, he was an ideal person to champion their cause, and he became heavily involved with their propaganda department. Such was his commitment and energy that, despite his essentially English background, he was selected to accompany the Irish delegation which travelled to London in October 1921, to meet the British

Prime Minister, Lloyd George. Lloyd George proposed that Ireland be split, with the south being granted independence, but the north remaining part of the Crown; Childers – ironically the most committed republican among the Irish party – was aghast, but Lloyd George threatened war if the Irish delegates did not accept, and faced with losing everything, they did.

The decision split the republican movement. A new, independent southern Ireland – the Irish Free State – came into being, but was bitterly opposed by those who insisted on nothing less than a united free Ireland. So intractable were the differences that a bitter civil war broke out, which claimed the lives of many of the heroes of the struggle, including Michael Collins himself.

Childers, too, was among them. His conscience would not allow him to accept the Free State, and he joined the republican forces. It seems that he did not take an active part in what proved a particularly nasty war, but master-minded their propaganda campaign. As such, he became an important target for Free State troops, and in November 1922 he was arrested. He had a small revolver in his pocket at the time – ironically a present from Michael Collins – and this was enough to condemn him under emergency laws enacted by the Free State.

During his brief period of imprisonment, there were many pleas to release him from his influential London and American contacts, but the authorities were clearly keen to make an example of such a high profile republican.

On 24 November 1922 Erskine Childers, author of *In the Ranks of the C.I.V.* and *The Riddle of the Sands*, perhaps the most unlikely of revolutionaries, was shot by a Free State firing squad.

Ian Knight
Canterbury
1999

IN THE RANKS

OF THE

C. I. V.

A NARRATIVE AND DIARY OF PERSONAL EXPERIENCES
WITH THE C.I.V. BATTERY (HONOURABLE ARTILLERY
COMPANY) IN SOUTH AFRICA

BY DRIVER

ERSKINE CHILDERS

CLERK IN THE HOUSE OF COMMONS

LONDON

SMITH, ELDER & CO., 15, WATERLOO PLACE

1901

DEDICATED

TO

MY FRIEND AND COMRADE

GUNNER BASIL WILLIAMS

CONTENTS.

IN THE RANKS OF THE C.I.V.

CHAPTER I.

THE "MONTFORT."

A wintry ride—Retrospect—Embarkation—A typical day—
"Stables" in rough weather—Las Palmas—The tropics—
Inoculation—Journalism—Fashions—"Intelligent anticipa-
tion"—Stable-guard—Arrival.

WITH some who left for the War it was "roses,
roses, all the way." For us, the scene was the
square of St. John's Wood Barracks at 2 A.M. on
the 3rd of February, a stormy winter's morning,
with three inches of snow on the ground, and
driving gusts of melting flakes lashing our
faces. In utter silence the long lines of horses
and cloaked riders filed out through the dimly-
lit gateway and into the empty streets, and we

B

were off at last on this long, strange journey
to distant Africa. Six crowded weeks were
behind us since the disastrous one of Colenso,
and with it the news of the formation of the
C.I.V., and the incorporation in that regiment
of a battery to be supplied by the Honourable
Artillery Company, with four quick-firing Vickers-
Maxim guns. Then came the hurried run over
from Ireland, the application for service, as a
driver, the week of suspense, the joy of success,
the brilliant scene of enlistment before the Lord
Mayor, and the abrupt change one raw January
morning from the ease and freedom of civilian
life, to the rigours and serfdom of a soldier's.
There followed a month of constant hard work,
riding-drill, gun-drill, stable work, and every sort
of manual labour, until the last details of the
mobilization were complete, uniforms and kit
received, the guns packed and despatched; and
all that remained was to ride our horses to the
Albert Docks; for our ship, the *Montfort*, was
to sail at mid-day.

Hardship had begun in earnest, for we had

thirteen miles to ride in the falling snow, and
our hands and feet were frozen. As we filed
through the silent streets, an occasional knot
of night-birds gave us a thin cheer, and once
a policeman rushed at me, and wrung my hand,
with a fervent "Safe home again!" White-
chapel was reached soon enough, but the
Commercial Road, and the line of docks, seemed
infinite.

However, at six we had reached the ship, and
lined up into a great shed, where we took off
and gave up saddles and head-collars, put on
canvas head-stalls, and then enjoyed an excellent breakfast, provided by some unknown
benefactor. Next we embarked the horses by
matted gangways (it took six men to heave my
roan on board), and ranged them down below
in their narrow stalls on the stable-deck.
Thence we crowded still further down to the
troop-deck—one large low-roofed room, edged
with rows of mess-tables. My entire personal
accommodation was a single iron hook in a
beam. This was my wardrobe, chest of drawers,

and an integral part of my bed; for from it
swung the hammock. We were packed almost
as thickly as the horses; and that is saying a
great deal. The morning was spent in fatigue
duties of all sorts, from which we snatched
furtive moments with our friends on the
crowded quay. For hours a stream of horses
and mules poured up the gangways; for two
other corps were to share the ship with us,
the Oxfordshire Yeomanry and the Irish Hospital. At two the last farewells had been said,
and we narrowed our thoughts once more to all
the minutiæ of routine. As it turned out, we
missed that tide, and did not start till two in the
next morning; but I was oblivious of such a
detail, having been made one of the two " stablemen " of my sub-division, a post which was to
last for a week, and kept me in constant attend-
ance on the horses down below; so that I might
just as well have been in a very stuffy stable on
shore, for all I saw of the run down Channel.
My duty was to draw forage from the forward
hold (a gloomy, giddy operation), be responsible

with my mate for the watering of all the
horses in my sub-division—thirty in number,
for preparing their feeds and " haying up" three
times a day, and for keeping our section of the
stable-deck swept and clean. We started with
very fine weather, and soon fell into our new
life, with, for me at least, a strange absence of
any sense of transition. The sea-life joined
naturally on to the barrack-life. Both are a
constant round of engrossing duties, in which
one has no time to feel new departures. The
transition had come earlier, with the first day in
barracks, and, indeed, was as great and sudden a
change, mentally and physically, as one could
possibly conceive. On the material side it was
sharp enough; but the mental change was
stranger still. There was no perspective left;
no planning of the future, no questioning of
the present; none of that free play of mind
and will with which we order our lives at home;
instead, utter abandonment to superior wills,
one's only concern the present point of time
and the moment's duty, whatever it might be.

This is how we spent the day.

The trumpet blew reveillé at six, and called us to early "stables," when the horses were fed and watered, and forage drawn. Breakfast was at seven : the food rough, but generally good. We were split up into messes of about fourteen, each of which elected two "mess orderlies," who drew the rations, washed up, swept the troop-deck, and were excused all other duties. I, and my friend Gunner Basil Williams, a colleague in my office at home, were together in the same mess. Coffee, bread and butter, and something of a dubious, hashy nature, were generally the fare at breakfast. I, as stableman, was constantly with the horses, but for the rest the next event was morning stables, about nine o'clock, which was a long and tedious business. The horses would be taken out of their stalls, and half of us would lead them round the stable-deck for exercise, while the rest took out the partitions and cleaned the stalls. Then ensued exciting scenes in getting them back again, an operation that most would not agree to without violent compulsion—and small blame to the poor brutes. It used to take our whole sub-division to shove my roan in. Each driver has two horses. My dun was a peaceful beast, but the roan was a by-word in the sub-division. When all was finished, and the horses fed and watered, it would be near 12.30, which was the dinner-hour. Some afternoons were free, but generally there would be more exercising and stall-cleaning, followed by the afternoon feeds and watering. At six came tea, and then all hands, including us stablemen, were free.

Hammocks were slung about seven, and it was one of the nightly problems to secure a place. I generally found mine under the hatchway, where it was airy, but in rainy weather moist. Then we were free to talk and smoke on deck till any hour. Before going to bed, I used to write my diary, down below, at a mess-table, where the lights shot dim rays through vistas of serried hammocks, while overhead the horses fidgeted and trampled in their stalls, making a distracting thunder on the iron decks. It was often writing under difficulties, crouching down with a hammock pressing on the top of one's head—the occupant protesting at the head with no excess of civility; a quality which, by the way, was very rare with us.

Soon after leaving the Bay, we had some rough weather. "Stables" used to be a comical function. My diary for the first rough day says:—"About six of us were there out of about thirty in my sub-division; our sergeant, usually an awesome personage to me, helpless as a babe, and white as a corpse, standing rigid. The lieutenant feebly told me to report when all horses were watered and feeds made up. It was a long job, and at the end I found him leaning limply against a stall. 'Horses all watered, and feeds ready, sir.' He turned on me a glazed eye, which saw nothing; then a glimmer of recollection flickered, and the lips framed the word 'feed,' no doubt through habit; but to pronounce that word at all under the circumstances was an effort of heroism for which I respected him. Rather a lonely day. My co-stable-man curled in a pathetic ball all day, among the hay, in our forage recess. My only view of the outer world is from a big port in this recess, which frames a square of heaving blue sea; but now and then one can get breathing-spaces on deck. In the afternoon —the ship rolling heavily—I went, by an order of the day before, to be vaccinated. Found the doctor on the saloon deck, in a long chair, very still. Thought he was dead, but saluted, and said what I had come for. With marvellous presence of mind, he collected himself, and said : ' I ordered six to come ; it is waste of lymph to do one only : get the other five.' After a short absence, I was back, reporting the other five not in a condition to do anything, even to be vaccinated. The ghost of a weary smile lit up the wan face. I saluted and left."

Our busy days passed quickly, and on the ninth of the month a lovely, still blue day, I ran up to look at the Grand Canary in sight on the starboard bow, and far to the westward the Peak of Teneriffe, its snowy cone flushed pink in the morning sun, above a bank of cloud. All was blotted out in two hours of stable squalors, but at midday we were anchored off Las Palmas (white houses backed by arid hills), the ill-fated *Denton Grange* lying stranded on the rocks, coal barges alongside, donkey engines chattering on deck, and a swarm of bum-boats round our sides, filled with tempting heaps of fruit, cigars, and tobacco. Baskets were slung up on deck, and they drove a roaring trade. A little vague news filtered down to the troop-deck; Ladysmith unrelieved, but Buller across the Tugela, and some foggy rumour about 120,000 more men being wanted. The Battery also received a four-footed recruit in the shape of a little grey monkey, the gift of the Oxfordshire Yeomanry. He was at once invested with the rank of Bombardier, and followed all our fortunes in camp and march and action till our return home. That day was a pleasant break in the monotony,

and also signalized my release from the office of
stableman. We were off again at six; an
exquisite night it was, a big moon in the
zenith, the evening star burning steadily over
the dim, receding island. We finished with a
sing-song on deck, a crooning, desultory per-
formance, with sleepy choruses, and a homely
beer-bottle passing from mouth to mouth.

Then came the tropics and the heat, and the
steamy doldrums, when the stable-deck was an
"Inferno," and exercising the horses like a
tread-mill in a Turkish bath, and stall-cleaning
an unspeakable business. Yet the hard work
kept us in fit condition, and gave zest to the
intervals of rest.

At this time many of us used to sling our
hammocks on deck, for down in the teeming
troop-deck it was suffocating. It was delicious
to lie in the cool night air, with only the
stars above, and your feet almost overhanging
the heaving sea, where it rustled away from
the vessel's sides. At dawn you would see
through sleepy eyes an exquisite sky, colouring

for sunrise, and just at reveillé the golden rim
would rise out of a still sea swimming and
shimmering in pink and opal.

Here is the diary of a Sunday :—

"*February* 11.—Reveillé at six. Delicious
bathe in the sail-bath. Church parade at ten ;
great cleaning and brushing up for it. Short
service, read by the Major, and two hymns. Then
a long lazy lie on deck with Williams, learning
Dutch from a distracting grammar by a pompous
old pedant. Pronunciation maddening, and the
explanations made it worse. Long afternoon,
too, doing the same. No exercising ; just water,
feed, and a little grooming at 4.30, then work
over for the day. Kept the ship lively combing
my roan's mane ; thought he would jump into
the engine-room. By the way, yesterday, when
waiting for his hay coming down the line, his
impatience caused him to jump half over the
breast-bar, bursting one head rope ; an extraordinary feat in view of the narrowness and
lowness of his stall. He hung in a nasty position for a minute, and then we got him to

struggle back. Another horse died in the night, and another very sick.

" Inoculation for enteric began to-day with a dozen fellows. Results rather alarming, as they all are collapsed already in hammocks, and one fainted on deck. It certainly is no trifle, and I shall watch their progress carefully. I can't be done myself for some days, as I was vaccinated two days ago (after the first unsuccessful attempt), in company with Williams. We went to the doctor's cabin on the upper deck, and afterwards sat on the deck in the sun to let our arms dry. After some consultation we decided to light a furtive cigarette, but were ignominiously caught by the doctor and rebuked. 'Back at school again,' I thought; 'caught smoking!' It seemed very funny, and we had a good laugh at it.

" It is a gorgeous, tropical night, not a cloud or feather of one ; a big moon, and dead-calm sea ; just a slight, even roll ; we have sat over pipes after tea, chatting of old days, and present things, and the mysterious future, sitting right aft on

the poop, with the moonlit wake creaming
astern."

Inoculation was general, and I was turned
off one morning with a joyous band of comrades,
retired to hammocks, and awaited the worst
with firmness. It was nothing more than a
splitting headache and shivering for about an
hour, during which time I wished Kruger,
Roberts, and the war at the bottom of the
sea. A painful stiffness then ensued, and that
was all. My only grievance was that two dying
horses were brought up and tied just below me,
and dosed—lucky beasts—with champagne by
their officer-owners! Also we had the hose
turned on us by some sailors, who were washing the boat-bridge above, and jeered at our
impotent remonstrances. In two days we were
fit for duty, and took our turn in ministering
to other sufferers.

We were a merry ship, for the men of our three
corps got on capitally together, and concerts and
amusements were frequent. They were held *al
fresco* on the forward deck, with the hammocks

of inoculates swinging above and around, so that these unfortunates, some of whom were pretty bad, had to take this strange musical medicine whether they liked it or no, and the mouth-organ band which attended on these occasions was by no means calculated to act as an opiate. Of course we had sports, both aquatic and athletic, and on the 18th Williams and I conceived the idea of publishing a newspaper; and without delay wrote, and posted up, an extravagant prospectus of the same. Helpers came, and ideas were plentiful. A most prolific poet knocked off poems "while you wait," and we soon had plenty of "copy." The difficulty lay in printing our paper. All we could do was to make four copies in manuscript, and that was labour enough. I am sure no paper ever went to press under such distracting conditions. The editorial room was a donkey engine, and the last sheets were copied one night among over-hanging hammocks, card-parties, supper-parties, and a braying concert by the Irish just overhead, by the light of an inch of candle. We pasted

up two copies on deck, sent one bound copy to
the officers, and the *Montfort Express* was a great
success. It was afterwards printed at Capetown.
Here is an extract which will throw some light
on our dress on board in the tropics :—

THE FEBRUARY FASHIONS.

By our Lady Correspondent.

" Dear Maude,

" I don't often write to you about
gentlemen's fashions, because, as a rule, they are
monstrously dull, but this season the stronger
sex seem really to be developing some originality.
Here are a few notes taken on the troopship
Montfort, where of course you know every
one is smart. (*Tout ce qu'il y a de plus Montfort*
has become quite a proverb, dear.) Generally
speaking, piquancy and coolness are the main
features. For instance, a neat costume for
stables is a pair of strong boots. To make this
rather more dressy for the dinner-table, a pair of
close-fitting pants may be added, but this is
optional. Shirts, if worn, are neutral in tint;
white ones are quite *démodé*. Vests are cut

low in the neck and with merely a suggestion of sleeve. Trousers (I blush to write it, dear) are worn baggy at the knee and very varied in pattern and colour, according to the tastes and occupation of the wearer. Caps *à la convict* are *de rigueur*. I believe this to spring from a delicate sense of sympathy with the many members of the aristocracy now in prison. The same chivalrous instinct shows itself in the fashion of close-cropped hair.

"There is a great latitude for individual taste ; one tall, handsome man (known to his friends, I believe, under the sobriquet of 'Kipper') is always seen in a delicious confection of some gauzy pink and blue material, which enhances rather than conceals the Apollo-like grace of his lissome limbs.

"At the Gymkhana the other day (a *very* smart affair), I saw Mr. 'Pat' Duffy, looking charmingly fresh and cool in a suit of blue tattooing, which I hear was made for him in Japan by a native lady.

"In Yeomanry circles, a single gold-rimmed

c

eye-glass is excessively *chic*, and, by the way, in the same set a pleasant folly is to wear a different coat every day.

"The saloon-deck is less interesting, because less variegated; but here is a note or two. Caps are usually *cerise*, trimmed with blue *passe-menterie*. To be really smart, the moustache must be waxed and curled upwards in corkscrew fashion. In the best Irish circles beards are occasionally worn, but it requires much individual distinction to carry off this daring innovation. And now, dear, I must say good-bye; but before I close my letter, here is a novel and piquant recipe for *Breakfast curry*: Catch some of yesterday's Irish stew, thoroughly disinfect, and dye to a warm khaki colour. Smoke slowly for six hours, and serve to taste.

"Your affectionate,

"NESTA."

Here is Williams on the wings of prophecy:—

OUR ARRIVAL IN CAPETOWN.

(*With Apologies to "Ouida."*)

"It was sunset in Table Bay—Phœbus' last

lingering rays were empurpling the beetling crags of Table Mountain's snowy peak—the great ship *Montfort*, big with the hopes of an Empire (on which the sun never sets), was gliding majestically to her moorings. Countless craft, manned by lissome blacks or tawny Hottentots, instantly shot forth from the crowded quays, and surged in picturesque disorder round the great hull, scarred by the ordure of ten score pure Arab chargers. 'Who goes there?' cried the ever-watchful sentry on the ship, as he ran out the ready-primed Vickers-Maxim from the port-hole. 'Speak, or I fire ten shots a minute.' 'God save the Queen,' was the ready response sent up from a thousand throats. 'Pass, friends,' said the sentry, as he unhitched the port companion-ladder. In a twinkling the snowy deck of the great transport was swarming with the dusky figures of the native bearers, who swiftly transferred the cargo from the groaning hold into the nimble bum-boats, and carried the large-limbed Anglo-Saxon heroes into luxurious

barges, stuffed with cushions soft enough to satisfy
the most jaded voluptuary. At shore, a sight
awaited them calculated to stir every instinct
of patriotism in their noble bosoms. On a
richly chased ebon throne sat the viceroy in
person, clad in all the panoply of power.
A delicate edge of starched white linen, a sight
which had not met their eyes for many a weary
week, peeped from beneath his gaudier accoutrements; the vice-regal diadem, blazing with the
recovered Kimberley diamond, encircled his brow,
while his finely chiselled hand grasped the great
sword of state. Around him were gathered a
dazzling bevy of all the wit and beauty of South
Africa; great chieftains from the fabled East,
Zulus, Matabeles, Limpopos and Umslopogaas,
clad in gorgeous scarlet feathers gave piquancy
to the proud throng. Most of England's wit
and manhood scintillated in the sunlight, while
British matrons and England's fairest maids lit
up with looks of proud affection; bosoms heaved
in sympathetic unison with the measured tramp
of the ammunition boots; bright eyes caught a

sympathetic fire from the clanking spurs of the
corporal rough-rider, while the bombardier in
command of the composite squadron of artillery,
horse-marines, and ambulance, could hardly pick
his way through the heaps of rose leaves scattered
before him by lily-white hands.   But the scene
was quickly changed, as if by enchantment.   At
a touch of the button by the viceroy's youngest
child, an urchin of three, thousands of Boer
prisoners, heavily laden with chains, brought
forward tables groaning with every conceivable
dainty.   The heroes set to with famished jaws,
and after the coffee, each negligently lit up his
priceless cigar with a bank-note, with the careless and open-handed improvidence so charming
and so characteristic of their profession.   But
suddenly their ease was rudely broken.   A
single drum-tap made known to all that the
enemy was at the gates.   In a moment the
commander had thrown away three parts of his
costly cigar, had sprung to his feet, and with
the heart of a lion and the voice of a dove, had
shouted the magical battle-cry, 'Attention!'

Then with a yell of stern resolve, and the answering cry of 'Stand easy, boys,' the whole squadron, gunners and adjutants, ambulance and bombardiers, yeomen and gentlemen farmers, marched forth into the night.

"That very night the bloody battle was fought which sealed the fate of the Transvaal—and the dashing colour-sergeant nailed England's proud banner on the citadel of Pretoria."

About once every week, it was my turn for stable-guard at night, consisting of two-hour spells, separated by four hours' rest. The drivers did this duty, while the gunners mounted guard over the magazines. On this subject I quote some nocturnal reflections from my diary:—
"Horses at night get very hungry, and have an annoying habit of eating one another's head-ropes reciprocally. When this happens you find chains if you can, and then they eat the framework of the stall. If you come up to protest, they pretend to be asleep, and eat your arm as you pass. They also have a playful

way of untying their breast-pads and standing
on them, and if you are conscientious, you can
amuse yourself by rescuing these articles from
under their hind feet."

The days were never very monotonous ; variety
was given by revolver practice, harness cleaning,
and lectures on first aid to the wounded. At
the same time it came as a great relief to hear
that we were at last close to the Cape.

From my diary :—

" *February* 26.—Heavy day at stables. Land
reported at eleven ; saw through forage-port a
distant line of mountains on port beam, edged
by a dazzling line of what looked like chalk cliffs,
but I suppose is sand. I am on stable-guard
for the night (writing this in the guard-room),
so when stables were over at four I had to pack
hard, and only got up for a glimpse of things at
five, then approaching Table Bay, guarded by
the splendid Table Mountain, with the table-
cloth of white clouds spread on it in the otherwise cloudless sky. I always imagined it a
smooth, dull mountain, but in fact it rises in

precipitous crags and ravines. A lovely scene as
we steamed up through a crowd of shipping—
transports, I suppose—and anchored some way
from shore. Blowing hard to-night. I have
been on deck for a few minutes. The sea is
like molten silver with phosphorescence under
the lash of the wind.

"*February* 27.—Tiresome day of waiting.
Gradually got known that we shan't land to-day,
though it is possible still we may to-night.
Torrid, windless day, and very hot work 'muck-
ing out' and tramping round with the horses,
which we did all the morning, and some of the
afternoon. News sent round that we had
captured Cronje and 5000 prisoners; all the
ships dressed with flags, and whistles blowing;
rockets in evening, banging off over my head
now, and horses jumping in unison. Shall we
be wanted? is the great question. We are
packed ready to land any minute."

CHAPTER II.

CAPETOWN AND STELLENBOSCH.

Landing—Green Point Camp—Getting into trim—My horses—
Interlude—Orders to march—Sorrows of a spare driver—March
to Stellenbosch—First bivouac—A week of dust and drill—The
road to water—Off again.

"*March 4.—Sunday.—Green Point Camp.—*
This is the first moment I have had to write in
since last Tuesday. I am on picket, and writing
in the guard-tent by a guttery lantern.

"To go back :—On Wednesday morning, the
28th of February, we steamed slowly up to a
great deserted quay. The silence struck me
curiously. I had imagined a scene of tumult
and bustle on the spot where troops in thousands
had been landing continuously for so long. We
soon realized that *we* were to supply all the
bustle, and that practical work had at last

begun, civilian assistance dispensed with, and
the Battery a self-sufficient unit. There was
not even a crane to help us, and we spent the
day in shoving, levering, and lifting on to
trucks and waggons our guns, carriages, limbers,
ammunition, and other stores, all packed as they
were in huge wooden cases. It was splendid
exercise as a change from stable-work. Weather
melting hot; but every one was in the highest
spirits; though we blundered tediously through
the job, for we had no experience in the fine
art of moving heavy weights by hand. I forgot
to take note of my sensations on first setting
foot on African soil, as I was groaning under a
case of something terribly heavy at the time.

"We worked till long after dark, slept like logs
in the dismantled troop-deck, rose early, and
went on until the afternoon of the next day,
when we landed the horses—of which, by the
way, we had only lost four on the voyage—
harnessed up some waggons to carry stores,
and were ready. While waiting to start, some
charming damsels in white muslin brought us

grapes. At about four we started for Green
Point Camp, which is on a big plain, between
the sea and Table Mountain, and is composed of
soft white sand, from which the grass has long
disappeared.

"Directly we reached it, the horses all flung
themselves down, and rolled in it. We passed
through several camps, and halted at our
allotted site, where we formed our lines and
picketed our horses heel and head. Then the
fun began, as they went wild, and tied themselves in strangulation knots, and kept it up all
night, as the sleepless pickets reported.

"After feeding and watering, we unloaded the
trucks which had begun to come in, ate some
bully-beef and bread, and then fell asleep
anyhow, in a confused heap in our tents. Mine
had thirteen in it, and once we were packed
no movement was possible."

For two more days we were busily employed
in unpacking stores, and putting the *materiel* of
battery into shape, while, at the same time, we

were receiving our complement of mules and
Kaffir drivers for our transport waggons. Then
came our first parades and drills. Rough we
were no doubt at first. The mobilization of a
volunteer battery cannot be carried out in an
instant, and presents numberless difficulties from
which infantry are free. Our horses were new
to the work, and a few of us men, including my
humble self, were only recent recruits.

The guns, too, were of a new pattern. The
H.A.C. at home is armed with the 15-pounder
guns in use in the Regular Field Artillery.
But for the campaign, as the C.I.V. Battery,
we had taken out new weapons (presented
by the City of London), in the shape of four
12½-pounder Vickers-Maxim field guns, taking
fixed ammunition, having practically no recoil,
and with a much improved breech-mechanism.
They turned out very good, but of course,
being experimental, required practice in han-
dling, which could not have been obtained in
the few weeks in the London barracks.

On the other hand, the large majority of us were

old hands, our senior officers and some of the
N.C.O.'s, either came direct from, or had pre-
viously served in, the Regular Horse Artillery,
and all ranks were animated by an intense desire
to reach the utmost efficiency at the earliest
possible moment.

My impressions of the next ten days are of
grooming, feeding, and exercising in the cool
twilight of dawn, sweltering dusty drills, often
in sand-storms, under a blazing mid-day sun, of
"fatigues" of all sorts, when we harnessed ourselves in teams to things, or made and un-made
mountains of ammunition boxes—a constant
round of sultry work, tempered by cool bathes
on white sand, grapes from peripatetic baskets,
and brief intervals of languid leisure, with *al
fresco* meals of bully-beef and dry bread outside
our tents.

Time was marked by the three daily stable
hours, each with their triple duty of grooming, feeding, and watering, the "trivial round"
which makes up so much of the life of a
driver. As a very humble representative of

that class, my horses were two " spares," that is,
not allotted to any team.   Much to my disgust,
I was not even provided with a saddle, and
had to do my work bareback, which filled me
with indignation at the time, but only makes
me smile now.   My roan was always a sort of
a pariah among the sub-division horses, an
incorrigible kicker and outcast, having to be
pickcted on a peg outside the lines for his
misdeeds.   Many a kick did I get from him;
and yet I always had a certain affection for
him in all his troubled, unloved life, till the
day when, nine months later, he trotted off
to the re-mount depôt at Pretoria, to vex some
strange driver in a strange battery.   My other
horse, a dun, was soon taken as a sergeant's
mount, and I had to take on an Argentine
re-mount, a rough, stupid little mare, with
kicking and biting propensities which quite
threw the roan's into the shade.   She also had
a peg of ignominy, and three times a day I had
to dance perilously round my precious pair with
a tentative body-brush and hoof-pick.   The

scene generally ended in the pegs coming away
from the loose sand, and a perspiring chase
through the lines. I had some practice, too,
in driving in a team, for one of our drivers
"went sick," and I took his place in the team
of an ammunition-waggon for several days.

Abrupt contrasts to the rough camp life were
some evenings spent with Williams in Capetown,
where it already felt very strange to be dining
at a table, and sitting on a chair, and using more
than one plate. Once it was at the invitation
of Amery of the *Times*, in the palatial splendour
of the Mount Nelson Hotel, where I felt
strangely incongruous in my by no means im-
maculate driver's uniform. But *how* I enjoyed
that dinner! Had there been many drivers
present, the management would have been
seriously embarrassed that evening.

Wildly varying rumours of our future used to
abound, but on March 14, a sudden order came
to raise camp, and march to Stellenbosch.
Teams were harnessed and hooked in, stores
packed in the buck waggons, tents struck, and

at twelve we were ready. Before starting Major McMicking addressed us, and said we were going to a disaffected district, and must be very careful. We took ourselves very seriously in those days, and instantly felt a sense of heightened importance. Then we started on the road which by slow, *very* slow, degrees was to bring us to Pretoria in August.

My preparations had been very simple, merely the securing of a blanket over the roan's distressingly bony spine, and putting a bit in his refractory mouth. As I anticipated, there had been a crisis over my lack of a saddle at the last moment, various officers and N.C.O.'s laying the blame, first on me (of all people), and then on each other, but chiefly on me, because it was safest. Not having yet learnt the unquestioning attitude of a soldier, I felt a great martyr at the time. The infinite insignificance of the comfort on horseback of one spare driver had not yet dawned upon me ; later on, I learnt that indispensable philosophy whose gist is, " Take what comes, and don't worry."

We passed through Capetown and its interminable suburbs, came out on to open rolling country, mostly covered with green scrub, and in the afternoon, formed our first regular marching camp, on a bit of green sward, which was a delicious contrast after Green Point Sand. Guns and waggons were marshalled, picket-ropes stretched between them, the horses tied up, and the routine of "stables" begun again.

It was our first bivouac in the open, and very well I slept, with my blanket and waterproof sheet, though it turned very cold about two with a heavy dew. A bare-backed ride of thirteen miles had made me pretty tired.

The next day we were up at five, for a march of eighteen miles to Stellenbosch. At mid-day we passed hundreds of re-mount ponies, travelling in droves, with Indian drivers in turbans and loose white linen. Half-way we watered our horses and had a fearful jostle with a Yeomanry corps (who were on the march with us), the Indians, and a whole tribe of mules which turned up from somewhere. In the afternoon

D

we arrived at our camp, a bare, dusty hill, parching under the sun.

We passed a week here, drilling and harness cleaning, in an atmosphere of dust and never-ending rumours.

Here are two days from my diary :—

" *March* 18.—Still here. Yesterday we rose early, struck tents, harnessed horses, and waited for orders to go to the station. Nothing happened : the day wore on, and in the evening we bivouacked as we were in the open. The night before we had great excitement about some mysterious signalling on the hills : supposed to be rebels, and the Yeomanry detachment (who are our escort) sent out patrols, who found nothing. To-day we are still awaiting orders, ready to start in half an hour, but they let us have a fine slack day, and we had a great bathe in the afternoon. Ostriches roam about this camp, eating empty soda-water bottles and any bridoon bits they can find. Three times a day we ride bareback to water horses at the re-mount depôt, passing picturesque Indian camps.

Williams and I are sitting under our ammunition waggon, where we are going to sleep: it is sunset and the hills are violet. A most gorgeous range of them fronts this camp.

"*March* 19.—Worse than ever. No orders to start, but orders to re-pitch tents. Delays seem hopeless, and now we may be any time here. Cooler weather and some rain to-day : much pleasanter. Only two tents to a sub-division, and there are sixteen in mine, a frightful squash. Long bareback ride for the whole battery before breakfast ; enjoyed it very much. Marching-order parade later. Argentine very troublesome : bites like a mad dog and kicks like a cow : can't be groomed. To-day she tried to bite me in the stomach, but as I had on a vest, shirt, body belt, money belt, and waistcoat, she didn't do much damage, and only got a waistcoat button and a bit of pocket ! "

We were uncommonly glad to receive definite orders on the 20th to move up country. The Battery was to be divided. The right section to go to Matjesfontein, and the left section, which was mine, to Piquetberg Road. Nobody knew where these places were, but we vaguely gathered that they were somewhere on the line of communications, which, rightly or wrongly, we thought very disappointing. For two more days we stood in readiness to start, chafing under countermanding orders, and pitching and re-pitching of tents, so little did we know then of the common lot of a soldier on active service.

We were to go by train, and the right section under the Major started about midnight on the 20th, and we on the next day, at four o'clock.

Guns, horses, and waggons were entrained very quickly, and just at dark I found myself in a second-class carriage, one of a merry party of eight, sitting knee-deep in belts, haversacks, blankets, cloaks, and water-bottles. We travelled on till midnight, and then stopped somewhere, posted guards, and slept in the carriages till dawn.

CHAPTER III.

PIQUETBERG ROAD.

Piquetberg Road—A fire—Kitless—A typical day—A bed—
"Stableman"—Picket—A rebel—Orders for the front, with
a proviso—Rain—An ungrateful patient—"Bazing"—Swimming horses—My work—The weather—A blue letter.

WHEN I woke up on the morning of the 22nd of
March, the legend "Piquetberg Road" was just
visible on a big white board opposite the carriage.
So this was our destination. There was a chill
sense in every one of not having got very far
towards the seat of war—indeed, we were scarcely
eighty miles from Capetown; but our spirits were
soon raised by the advent of some Tommies of the
Middlesex Militia, who spoke largely of formid-
able bodies of rebels in the neighbourhood, of
an important pass to guard, and of mysterious
strategical movements in the near future; so

that we felt cheerful enough as we detrained
our guns and horses, harnessed up, and marched
over a mile and a half of scrub-clothed *veldt*, to
the base of some steep hills, where we pitched
our camp, and set to work to clear the ground
of undergrowth.   We were at the edge of a
great valley, through which ran the line of
railway, disappearing behind us in a deep gorge
in the hills, where a little river ran.   This was
the pass we were to help to guard.

Below in the valley lay a few white houses
round the station, a farm or two dotted the distant
slopes, and the rest was desert scrub and veldt.

Now that the right section had parted from
us, we had two officers, Captain Budworth commanding, and Lieutenant Bayley ; about sixty
men, two guns, two ammunition waggons, and
two transport waggons, with their mules and
Kaffir drivers, under a conductor.   Our little
square camp was only a spot upon the hill-side,
the guns and horse-lines in the middle, a tent
for the officers on one side, and a tent at each
corner for the men.   Here we settled down to the

business-like routine of camp life, with great hopes of soon being thought worthy to join a brigade in the field.

The work was hard enough, but to any one with healthy instincts the splendid open-air life was very pleasant. Here are some days from my diary :—

" *March* 23.—Marching order parade. Drove centres of our sub-division waggon.

" I have got a saddle for my own horse at last, and feel happier. Where it came from I don't know.

" I am 'stableman' for three days, and so missed a bathing parade to-day, which is a nuisance, as there is no means of washing here nearer than a river some distance off, to which the others rode. While they were away there was an alarm of fire in the lines of the Middlesex Militia, next to ours. Bugles blew the 'alarm.' The scrub had caught fire quite near the tents, and to windward of us. There were only four of us in camp, one a bombardier, who took command and lost his head, and after some wildly contradictory orders, said to me, ' Take that gun to a place of safety.' How he expected me to take the gun by myself I don't know. However, the fire went out, and all was well.

" I forgot to say that on the day we left Stellenbosch, a mail at last came in, and I got my first letters. They came by the last mail, and we have evidently missed a lot. Also a telegram, weeks old, saying Henry (my brother) had joined Strathcona's Horse in Ottawa and was coming out here. Delighted to hear it, but I shall probably never see him.

" By the way, I am parted from all my kit at present. Having had no saddle, I have been used to put it on the transport waggon of our sub-division, but this went with the other section for some inscrutable reason, or rather didn't go, for it was wrecked by a train when crossing the line. I heard vaguely that the contents were saved and sent on with the right section, but am quite prepared to find it is lost. Not that I miss it much. One wants very little really, in this sort of life. Fortunately I kept back my

cloak and blanket. A lovely night to-night:
Williams and I have given up tents as too
crowded, and sleep under the gun; to-night
we have built a rampart of scrub round it, as
there is a fresh wind.

"*March* 28.—Marching order parade at eight.
I was told to turn out as a mounted gunner,
which is a very jolly job. You have a single
mount and ride about as ground-scout, advance-
guard, rear-guard, etc. We had a route-march
over the pass through the mountains, a lovely
ride, reminding me of the Dordogne. We came
out into a beautiful valley the other side, with a
camp of some Highlanders : here we fed and
watered ourselves and horses and then marched
home. My kit turned up from Matjesfontein.

"It strikes me that I have given very few
actual details of our life and work, so, as I have
got two hours to myself, I will try and do it
more exactly.

"Reveillé sounds at 5.30, and 'stables' at
six, with the first gleam of dawn ; horses are
now fed, and then groomed for half an hour.

From this point the days differ. Here is the sketch of a marching order day, from a driver's point of view. To resume, then :—From 6.30 we have half an hour to pack kits, that is to say, to roll the cloak and strap it on the riding saddle, pack the off saddle with spare boots and rolls made up of a waterproof sheet, blanket, harness-sheets, spare breeches, muzzles, hay-nets, etc., and finally to buckle on filled nose-bags and our mess-tins, and strap horse-blankets under the saddles. His stable-kit and the rest of a driver's personal belongings are carried in four wallets, two on each saddle.

" At seven, breakfast—porridge, coffee, and bread, and sometimes jam. Our tent has a mess-subscription, and adds any extras required from the canteen. But we always fare well enough without this, for the Captain thinks as much of the men as of the horses, and is often to be seen tasting and criticizing at the cooks' fire.

" At 7.30 ' boot and saddle' sounds, and in half an hour your horses have to be ready-harnessed and yourself dressed in ' marching order,' that is to say, wearing helmet, gaiters, belt, revolver, haversack, water-bottle, and leg-guard.

"At eight 'hook in' is ordered; teams are hooked together and into the guns and waggons. 'Mount the detachment' and gunners take their seats. 'Prepare to mount' (to the drivers) followed by 'Mount,' 'Walk March,' and you are off. We always go first to the watering-place, a sandy pool in the river, unhook and water the horses. Then we either march away, and drill and exercise over the veldt, or go for a route-march to some distance. The weather is always hot, and often there is a dust-storm raging, filling eyes, ears, and mouth, and trying the temper sorely.

"We are back at camp about 1.30, form our lines again, between the guns and waggons, unharness, rub down horses, and then have dinner. There is fresh beef generally (that unlovely soldiers' stew), and either rice, duff, or, now and then, stewed quinces, which are very common in the country. We can buy beer at a canteen, or, better still, draught ginger-beer, which is a grand drink. At three 'stables' sounds, with grooming first, and then (I am choosing a full day) harness cleaning; that is to say, soaping all leather-work, and scouring steel-work. Harness-cleaning is irksome work, and, as far as appearances go, is a heart-breaking task, for the eternal dust is always obliterating every trace of one's labour. I have none of my own to look after yet, but help the others.

"At 4.30 or five 'Prepare for water' sounds. You put a bridoon on one horse, and, if you are luxurious, a blanket and surcingle to sit on, lead the other, and form up in a line; then 'file right' is the order, and you march off to the watering place, wearing any sort of costume you please. And very slight and *negligé* some of them are. In the cool of the evening, this is a very pleasant three quarters of an hour. After watering comes the evening feed, followed by tea at six o'clock, and then the day's work is done."

The evenings in that climate are delicious ; we could sit in our shirt-sleeves until any hour, without any perceptible chill in the air, playing cards, or smoking and talking, or reading by a lantern. Williams and I found picquet a great resource ; and many a good game of whist have I had sitting in a crowded quartette in our ramshackle battery Cape-cart, with an inch of candle guttering among the cards.

Most of us slept in the tents, but I preferred the open, even in dust-storms, when choosing a site required some skill. The composition of a bed was a question of sacks. There was one very large variety of chaff-sack, which was a sleeping-bag in itself ; with this and your blanket and cloak, and under the lee of some forage or scrub, you could defy anything. The only peril was that of a loose horse walking on you.

On some afternoons we were quite free till the stable-hour at four. Till then we could bask in camp, or go for a bathe in the river, where there was one splendid deep-water pool, whence you could hear the baboons barking on the hill-sides, and see the supply trains for the front grinding heavily up the pass.

Rumours of a move never lost their charm. At first we used to take them seriously, but gradually the sense of permanence began to pervade our camp. Solid tin shelters rose for the guard and the sergeants; a substantial tin canteen was erected close to the lines by cynical provision-dealers. Those visionary rebels declined to show themselves; nobody attacked our precious pass; and, in short, we had to concentrate our minds upon the narrow circle of our daily life.

A recurring duty for drivers was that of " stableman." There were two of these for each sub-division, who were on duty for the whole day in the lines. Their function, in addition to the usual duties, was to draw forage, watch the horses, and prepare all the feeds in the nose-bags, ready for the drivers. The post was no sinecure, for in addition to the three standard oat feeds, there was oat straw to be put down after dinner, and, at eight o'clock at night, a final supper of

chaff, except for invalids, who got special feeds. A
list of these was given you generally at the last
moment, and it was a test for your temper to go
round the lines on a windy night, lighting many
futile matches, in order. to see the number on
the off fore hoof, so as to hit off the right ones.
There was generally a nose-bag missing at this
stage, which was ultimately found on a C horse
(my sub-division was D), and then there was a
lively five minutes of polite recrimination. At
8.30 the nose-bags had to be taken off, and
muzzles put on—canvas affairs with a leather
bottom, strapped on by the head collar—as a
preventive against disease from the chill morning
air. Every man, after evening stables, was supposed to leave his muzzles on the jowl-piece of
his horses, but a stableman was quite sure to
find two missing, and then he would have to
scour the tents, and drive the offender to the
lines to repair his neglect; then he could go to
bed. Another extra duty was that of picket at
night, which came round to gunners and drivers
alike, about every ten days. " Two hours on and

four hours off" was the rule, as on all sentry-
duty. I rarely found the night watches long.
There was plenty to do in watching the horses,
which are marvellously ingenious at untying
knots, and in patrolling the camp on the look-out
for imaginary rebels. By the way, the only live
rebel I ever saw was the owner of a farm, near
which we halted during one sultry dusty route-
march. He refused to allow us to water our
horses and ourselves at his pond, defying us
with Lord Kitchener's proclamation enjoining
" kind treatment " of the Dutch !

As the days passed without orders for the
front, impatience and disappointment grew. We
were fit and well, and were not long in reaching
the standard of efficiency which carried us
successfully through our campaigning later. We
used to " grouse " vigorously over our bad luck,
with what justice I do not pretend to say ; but
no one who has not experienced it, can understand the bitterness of inaction, while the stream
of reinforcements is pouring to the front. Scraps
of news used to come in of the victorious march

of the army northward, and of the gallant behaviour of the C.I.V. Infantry. Companies of Yeomanry used to arrive, and leave for destinations with enticing names that smelt of war, and night after night rollicking snatches of " Soldiers of the Queen " would float across the valley from the troop-trains, as they climbed the pass northward.

As early as April 15th, the word went round that we were under orders to go to Bloemfontein —" as soon as transport could be ready for us."

" *April* 15.—Amid great delight the Captain to-day read a telegram saying we are to go to Bloemfontein as soon as the railway can take us We had just come in from the ride to water in drenching rain and ankle deep in mud, but a great cheer went up. The railway limitation is a rather serious one, as I believe the line is in a hopeless state of block; but we'll hope for the best. The rainy season has begun in the most unmistakable fashion. It has poured so far in buckets for twenty-four hours; I slept out last night, but daren't to-night; outlying parts of

E

me got wet, in spite of the waterproof over me.
Thank goodness, we have good boots, gaiters, and
cloaks.   We rode to water at eleven in various
queer costumes, and mostly bare legs, and
afterwards dug trenches through the lines.   The
rest of the day we have been huddled in a heap
in our tent, a merry crowd, taking our meals
in horrible discomfort, but uproarious spirits.

"I still have the roan, but have lost the Argentine and got a bay mare instead ; it's not a bad
animal.   There was a false alarm of glanders
the other day.   One of the gun-team had a
swollen throat, but it turns out to be something
else.   I was told off to help foment him with
hot water the night it was discovered.   He
kicked us all, and completely floored me with a
kick in the chest, which didn't hurt happily.
Yesterday I had to take him down to the
station and foment him from the kitchen boiler
of the station-master's wife.   I enjoyed it, as I
had plenty of rests, and the station-master's wife
made me delicious tea, served to me by a sweet
little white-frocked girl.   By the way, on the

road to water the other day a caravan full of
people stopped us, and small maidens went down
the line, giving us apples and cigarettes and
cakes."

Little we understood that ironical "railway"
proviso of a harassed general staff. We had been
reviewed the day before, and the good practice
of our guns had been praised by the inspecting
officer. Now was our chance, we thought.
Nevertheless, we had to live on that guarded
"order" for another month.

But in spite of our disappointment I believe
all of us will look back with real pleasure to
that time. There was no monotony in the life,
thanks to our officers, who continually introduced variety into our work. "Marching
order" days were the commonest; but there
were others of a lighter sort. On one day we
would go for a long expedition in drill-order
with the guns, taking cooks and our dinner with
us, and have what we used to call a picnic by
some pleasant river-side. On another the guns
would be left at home, and we would ride out

for exercise, often through the pass, which led
through a lovely ravine to a pretty little place
called Tulbagh, where there was another small
camp of troops. Sometimes " bazing " was the
order, a portmanteau-word describing a morning spent in grazing the horses, and bathing ourselves. My diary of April 8th says, " Yesterday about twenty of us went out to practice
swimming with horses. We rode about seven
miles to a deepish river, stripped, off-saddled,
and swam them across. Some wouldn't do it at
all, but most of them swam across and back.
You buckle the rein up short and leave him
alone. It's a very queer motion at first. One
of those I took declined to go in, in spite of half
a dozen chaps goading him on in various ways,
and finally bolted away over the veldt, carrying
me naked. He soon came back though. The
horses have got the habit now of sticking
together, and if they get loose in camp never
leave the lines. It is a nuisance sometimes, if
you have to act as a single mount, and ride
away on some errand. My Argentine greatly

resents such a move, and tries to circle like a clockwork mouse. She has grown as fat as a pig, though some horses are doing poorly. The oats are of a very bad quality."

That brings me to my horses and my own work. We all of us changed horses a good deal in those days, and I and the roan had several partings and re-unitings. As a spare driver, my own work was very varied, now of driving in a team, now of riding spare horses, and occasion-ally of acting as a mounted gunner. Williams was a regular mounted gunner, his mount being a wicked, disreputable-looking little Argentine (called "Pussy" (with a lisp) for her qualities), to whom he owed three days in hospital at one time from a bad kick, but whom he ended by transforming into as smart and peaceable a little mount as you could find. My own chance came at last; and when about the end of April one of our drivers was sent home sick, I took his place as centre driver of an ammunition waggon, and kept it permanently. I said good-bye to the

roan and Argentine, and took over a fine pair
of bays.

My chief impression of the weather is that of
heat and dust, but there were times when we
thought the dreaded rainy season had begun;
when the camp was a running morass, and we
crouched in our tents, watching pools of water
soaking under our harness sheets, and counting
the labour over rusted steel. But it used to
pass off, leaving a wonderful effect; every waste
oat seed about the camp sprouted; little green
lawns sprang up in a single night round the
places where the forage was heaped, and the
whole veldt put on a delicate pink dress, a
powder of tiny pink flowers.

By the middle of May we began to think we
had been forgotten altogether, but at last, on
the morning of the 17th of May, as we were
marching out to drill, an orderly galloped up,
and put a long blue letter into the Captain's
hand. We had seen this happen before, and our
discussions of the circumstance, as we rode along,
were sceptical, but this time we were wrong.

CHAPTER IV.

BLOEMFONTEIN.

The railway north—Yesterday's start—Travelling made easy—
Feeding horses—A menu—De Aar—A new climate—Naauwport—Over the frontier—Bloemfontein—A fiasco—To camp
again—The right section—Diary days—Riding exercise—A
bit of history—Langman's Hospital—The watering-place—
Artillery at drill—A review—A camp rumour—A taste of
freedom—A tent scene.

FROM my diary :—

" *May* 20.—*Sunday.*—I write this on the train,
on the way up north, somewhere near Beaufort
West ; for the long-wished day has come at last,
and we are being sent to Kroonstadt, which
anyway is pretty near to, if not actually at,
the front. Our only fear is now that it will be
too late. All day the train has been traversing,
the Karoo, a desert seamed by bare rocky
mountains, and without a sign of life on it,

only vast stretches of pebbly soil, dotted sparsely with dusty-green dwarf scrub. But to go back. We started yesterday. All went smoothly and simply. At eight, kit was inspected; in the morning, bareback exercise; at twelve, tents struck; at 12.30 dinner; at one, 'boot and saddle.' When we were hooked in and mounted, the Captain made a splendid little speech in the incisive forcible voice we had learned to know so well, saying we had had for long the most trying experience that can befall a soldier, that of standing fast, while he sees his comrades passing him up to the front. He congratulated us on the way we had met that experience. There had been no complaining or slackness in our work on that account. He hoped we would have the luck to go into action, and his last advice to us was 'to keep our stomachs full and our bellies warm!'

"Then we marched to the station, unharnessed, packed harness, boxed the horses, put the guns and waggons on the trucks, and were ready.

But the train didn't start till about eight o'clock
in the evening. One box was reserved for
kickers, and you should have seen their disgust
when they found nothing to bully! We had,
and have, a vague idea that the journey was
to last about a week, so Williams and I bought
a large box of provisions and a small paraffin
stove. Accustomed to delays, we quite expected
no engine to turn up or something like that, but
finally a whistle blew and we were off, and a
delirious shout went up, and then we all sighed
with relief, and then got doubly merry, shouting
vain things over a long untasted beverage,
whisky and water. One hears so much about
the horrors of war that I scarcely dare to describe
the men's accommodation on board this train.
It is strange, but true, that I have never travelled
more comfortably in my life, and probably never
shall. Most compartments have only four men
to them, and by great good luck, and a little
diplomacy, Williams and I have one to ourselves,
though we form our mess with the four chaps
in the next one. Now the beauty of it is that

no one can get into our train, so, if you get out
at a station, you need have no fear of finding a
nurse with twins in your special corner seat.
You live without these terrors, and have room
to stretch, and sleep, and read, and have meals,
with no one to ask you to show your ticket.
In fact, things are reversed; we are not
herded and led, and snubbed by porters and
officials, but the train belongs to us, and we
ignore them.

"We sat up late last night, and then Williams
and I slept in great comfort, though it felt quite
odd to have something between one and the
stars. It's true there was a slight break,
caused by the door being flung open, and sacks
of bread being hustled in from the outside. But
a soldier's training takes no account of these
things, and you instinctively jump out half-
dressed, and help to shovel more sacks in, you
don't know why, or what they are. Being
woken up, we got on to the platform over an
intervening train, and sent cables home from an
office standing invitingly open. Then to bed

again. Later, in my dreams, I was aware of a
sergeant and an irascible little station-master
coming into the carriage with lanterns and
throwing most of the sacks out again, which it
seemed had been annexed feloniously by our
Captain, at the last station, in his zeal to keep
our 'stomachs full.' I was glad to get rid of the
sacks, as they filled our carriage up completely.
The train has to stop for about three-quarters of
an hour or less, three times a day, for feeding and
watering the horses. The first stop to-day was
about 6.30 A.M. We tumbled out in the delicious
fresh air, and formed into pre-arranged feeding
and watering parties. I am on the feed party
of our subdivision, and we climbed like beetles
up the sides of the trucks, which are open, and
strap on the nose-bags. Then we washed at a
friendly tap, and had our own breakfast which
the cooks had cooked—coffee and porridge. Then
we climbed back and took off nose-bags, and then
the train went on. At this station we 'commandeered' a splendid table in the shape of a
large square tin advertisement of a certain

Scotch whisky, and played whist on it after breakfast. The train wound slowly through a barren stretch of brown plain and rocky wild. Stations happened now and then, little silent spots in the wilderness, their *raison d'être* a mystery, no houses, roads, or living things near, except a white tent or two, and some sunburnt men in khaki looking curiously at us. There are troops in small bodies all up the line in this 'loyal' colony. At one station the Kimberley mail caught us up, and the people threw us magazines and biscuits from the windows. All engines and stations were decorated with flags in honour of the relief of Mafeking, the news of which came through yesterday. A hospital train bound to Capetown also passed, with some pale faces and bandaged limbs in evidence.

" At 1.30 we stopped again for feed and water, and when we went on our mess sat down to the following lunch, which I think does credit to our catering powers.

MENU.

R. B. S.

Emergency Soup.

Cold Roast Fowl, with Stuffing.

Bully Beef, with Mustard.

Whiskied Biscuits.

Desserts Variés. Chocolate. Ginger. Bonbons. Oranges.

German Beer.

Cigars.   Cigarettes.

" I wrote the *menu* out in French first, but it seemed not to suit.

" All the afternoon the same desolation, like pictures one sees of the moon's surface. About six, water and feed at Beaufort West, and horses led out, trucks mucked out, and tea served out.

" The night was very cold; in fact, the climate is quite different on these high table-lands. I woke up about six, looked out, and saw, just opposite, the legend DE AAR, which for the first time seemed to connect us with the war. We stopped a moment, and then moved on through lines of tents, loaded waggons, mountains of ammunition, etc. Then I saw a strange sight, in the shape of ice on puddles and white hoar-frost. Soon out on the broad, brown veldt,

far-distant hills showing finely cut in the exquisitely clear air.   Such an atmosphere I have
never seen for purity.   The sun was rising into
a cloudless sky from behind a kopje.   The flat-
topped kopje is now the regular feature.   They
are just like miniature Table-mountains, and it
is easy to see how hard to capture they must be.
Water, feed, and breakfast at a tiny roadside
place, with the inevitable couple of tents and
khaki men.   We were at whist when we steamed
up to a big, busy camp-station, the Red Cross
flying over a dozen big marquee tents, and a
couple of hundred sorry-looking remounts (by
the look of them) picketed near.   This was
Naauwport.   We stopped alongside a Red Cross
train full of white, unshaven faces—enterics and
wounded going back to the base.   They were
cheerful enough, and we shouted inquiries about
one another.   They were unanimous in saying
we were too late, which was very depressing news,
but I don't suppose they knew much about it.
We washed ourselves in big buckets here.   As
we were steaming out I saw a long unfamiliar

sight, in the shape of a wholesome, sunburnt
English girl, dressed in short-skirted blue serge,
stepping out as only an English girl can. She
was steering for the Red Cross over the tents,
and, I daresay, was nursing there. Off again, over
the same country, but looking more inhabited ;
passed several ostrich farms, with groups of the
big, graceful birds walking delicately about ;
also some herds of cattle, and a distant farm or
two, white against the blue hill-shadows. Soon
came the first visible signs of war—graves, and
long lines of trenches here and there. At a
stop at a shanty (can't call it a station) a man
described a fight for a kopje just by the railway.
Coleskop was in view, a tall, flat-topped mountain, and later we steamed into the oft-taken
and retaken Colesberg Junction, and were shown
the hill where the Suffolks were cut up. All
was now barren veldt again, and the strangeness
of the whole thing struck me curiously. Why
should men be fighting here ? There seemed
to be nothing to fight for, and nothing behind
to get to when you had fought.

" *May* 22.—*Tuesday.*—As I write we are standing just outside Bloemfontein ; cold, sunny morning ; the Kaffir quarter just on our right, a hideous collection of mud houses with tin roofs ; camps and stores on the left ; boundless breadth of veldt beyond ; the town in front under a long, low kopje, a quiet, pretty little place.

" We reached the frontier—Norval's Pont—at 6 P.M. yesterday, and after a long delay, moved slowly out in the dark, till the shimmer of water between iron girders told us we were crossing the Orange river. Once off the bridge, a shout went up for our first step on the enemy's country. Then all went on the same. We made ourselves comfortable, and brewed hot cocoa, for all the world as though we were travelling from Boulogne to Geneva. The only signs of hostility were the shrill execrations of a crowd of infant aborigines.

' We woke up to a changed country. The distances were still greater, low hills only occasionally breaking the monotony of flat plain, but

the scrub had given way to grass, not verdant
Irish grass, but sparse, yellow herbage. Ant-hills
and dead horses were the only objects in the
foreground, except eternal wreaths and tangles
of telegraph wire along the tracks, and piles
of sleepers, showing the damage done, and now
repaired, to line and wire. The same pure
crisp air and gentle sunlight.

"*May* 24.—*Thursday*.—I write in our tent on
the plateau above Bloemfontein, and will go on
where I left off on the 22nd. To our utter disgust, after standing for hours in a siding of the
station, chatting to all sorts and conditions of the
species soldier, the order came to detrain. We
drivers took the horses first to water, and then
picketed them on an arid patch of ground near the
station, where the gunners had meantime brought
the guns and waggons. It was now dark, and
there were no rations served out; very cold, too,
and we had no kit, but it wasn't these things we
minded, but the getting out instead of training
on. 'Kroonstadt' is redolent of war, but,
'Bloemfontein' spells inaction. However, there

F

was no help for it. We slept on the ground, and precious cold this new climate was. I hadn't my Stohwasser blanket, and spent most of the night stamping about and smoking. At reveillé next day rations were still lacking, but we all trooped off to a tin hut and had tea, given by an unseen angel, named Sister Bagot. 'Boot and saddle' sounded at nine, and we marched off to the camp, about two miles away. There was a very nasty ravine to cross, and we had to have drag ropes on behind, with the gunners on them, to steady us down the descent. I was driving centres as usual, and saw the leaders almost disappear in front of me. At the bottom we crossed a stream, and then galloped them up the other side. Soon after we passed through Bloemfontein, a quiet, dull-looking place, like a suburb of Cape Town, mounted a long hill, and came out on to another broad plain, kopjes in the distance, and tents dotted far and wide. The first moving thing I saw was a funeral,—slow music, a group of khaki figures, and the bright colours of a Union Jack glinting between.

" Our right section, that is, the other half of the Battery, from which we had been separated ever since Stellenbosch, had trained on a day ahead of us, and were now already encamped, so we marched up and joined our lines to theirs, pitched our tents, and once more the Battery was united. And what a curious meeting it was! Half of them were unrecognizable with beards and sunburn, as were many of us, I suppose. What yarns we had! All that day, in the intervals between fatigues, and far into the night, in the humming tents. Jacko was with them. He had been lost on the journey, but came on by a later train very independently."

We all had a presentiment of evil, and, as it turned out, we were kept nearly a month at Bloemfontein, while still reports of victories came in. Yet news was very scarce, and had we known it, the period was only just beginning, of that long, irregular warfare, by which the two provinces had to be conquered, when the brilliancy of Roberts's meteoric march to

Pretoria was past. We were to take our small share in work as necessary and arduous as any in these latter stages of the war.

Meanwhile we were now a complete battery, and worked hard at our drill as such, though there was very little to learn after our long training in Cape Colony. We kept our spirits up, though the time was a depressing one. Mortality was high in Bloemfontein at that time, in spite of the healthy, exhilarating climate. A good many of us had to go into hospital, but we were fortunate enough to lose no lives through illness.

Here are some extracts from my diary :—

"*May* 24.—*Queen's Birthday.*—The guns went to a review, and got high praise for their turn out. The rest of us exercised on stripped saddles, trotting over bare flat ground, with sparse grass on it, the greatest contrast to the Piquetberg Road country.

"In the evening Williams and I and some others wandered off to try and get a wash. We prowled over the plain and among the camps asking the way to water, and carrying our towels and soap, and finally stumbled over a trough and a tap. The water here is unfit for drinking, and we are forbidden to drink it except boiled.

"*May* 28.—Riding exercise again; a long and jolly ride round the country. Half-way we did cavalry exercises for some time, which, when every man has a led horse, and many two of them, is rather a rough game. I was riding Williams's Argentine, Pussy, a game little beast, but she got very worried and annoyed over wheeling and forming fours and sections. Directly we got back and had off-saddled we fell in, and one out of four was allowed to go down to town and see the Proclamation of Annexation read. I was lucky enough to be picked, tumbled into proper dress, and hurried down just in time. The usual sight as I passed the cemetery, thirteen still forms on stretchers in front of the gate, wrapped in the rough service blanket, waiting to be buried. I found the Market Square full of troops drawn up, and a flag-staff in the middle, with a rolled-up flag on it. Soon a band heralded the arrival of the Governor, Colonel Pretyman, and the Staff-officers. Then a distant voice began the Proclamation, of which I couldn't hear a word except 'colony' at the end, at which every one cheered. Then the flag was unrolled, and hung dead for a minute, till a breeze came and blew out 'that haughty scroll of gold,' the Royal Standard. Bands struck up 'God save the Queen,' a battery on a hill above the town thundered out a royal salute, everybody cheered, and I was standing on British soil. I saw not a single native Dutchman about, only crowds of the khakied of all ranks and sorts. After this little bit of history-making I hurried back to the commonplace task of clipping my mare's heels, an operation requiring great agility on the part of the clipper.

"For a 'stableman,' as I am now, the evening is rather a busy one. At seven you have to make up the feeds for the last feed; at 7.45 put them round the harness-sets behind the horses; at eight feed, for which all hands turn out ; at 8.30 take off nose-bags and put on muzzles ; and after that make up another feed ready for early next morning. You can't finish before 'lights out,' and have to go to bed in the dark, to the loudly expressed annoyance of your neighbours in the tent (I sleep in a tent these nights), on whose bodies you place the various articles of your kit while you arrange your bed, and whose limbs you sometimes mistake for materials for a pillow, when you are composing that important piece of upholstery.

"*May* 30.—*Wednesday.*—In the afternoon Williams and I went to visit a friend in Langman's Hospital. Bloemfontein is a town of hospitals, red crosses flying at every turn. The mortality is high, even, I was surprised to hear from our friend, among sisters and hospital orderlies. Out of six sisters in his hospital, which seemed a very good one, four had enteric at the time, and one had died of it. I was on picket duty this night, and had a lively time chasing loose horses in the dark. A new sort of

head-rope we are using seems very palatable to
the horses, as they mostly eat it for supper, and
then get loose.

"*May* 31.—Out at riding exercise we came to
a fortified kopje, where we dismounted, and
were allowed to examine a beautifully made
·trench running round the top, very deep, and
edged by a wall of stones arranged to give
loopholes.   Some one found a Boer diary in
the dust, the entries in which seemed to alter-
nate between beer and Bible-reading.   We
always water at the common trough, the last
thing before return.   Such varieties of the
horse species you could see no where else ; thick,
obstinate little Argentines, all with the same
Roman noses and broad, ugly heads ; squab
little Basuto ponies, angular skeletonesque Cape
horses, mules of every nationality, Texan,
Italian, Illyrian, Spanish ; here and there a
beautiful Arab belonging to some officer ; and
dominating all, our own honest, substantial 'bus
and tram horses, almost the only representatives
of English horseflesh.   There are always a few

detached horses stampeding round ownerless, or limping feebly down with a lost, hopeless look in their eyes, tripping at every step over a tattered head-rope, and seeming to belong to nobody and care for nothing. We always ride down in strict order, each man leading one or two.

"*June* 3.—Marching-order parade. We had a good morning drill over what is perfect artillery country, with just the right amount of excitement in the shape of ditches to jump, and ant-hills, which are legion, and holes to avoid. I am delighted with my pair, which are both very fit now; and our waggon team has been going very well.

"*June* 4.—Riding exercise and sham-fight; an enemy supposed to be attacking a convoy. Being in the convoy, I haven't a clear idea of what happened, but only know we were kept dodging about kopjes, and bolting across open places uncaptured.

"*June* 5.—Another field-day, with guns and waggons, before Colonel Davidson, the Brigadier of Artillery here. We went out to some distant kopjes, and went into action at two different points. I believe the shooting was very good; they had targets of biscuit-tins stuck up on the kopjes. Some of you who read this at home may not know how artillery work, so I may as well roughly sketch what happens on these occasions. There are four guns and five waggons. A waggon is built on the same plan as a gun, that is, in two parts, the waggon-body and the waggon-limber, the limber being in front, and having the pole for draught, just as the gun-carriage and the gun-limber form the two parts of the 'gun.' Both waggon-body and waggon-limber carry ammunition, as does the gun-limber. There are four gunners on the gun, and four on the waggon. When suitable ground has been selected by the Major, and thoroughly scouted first by the mounted gunners, the order is given to advance into action. The guns trot up in line; 'Action front' is given; each team immediately makes a right-about wheel on its own ground, thus bringing the muzzle of the gun to the front. The limber is

then unhooked from the trail of the gun, and
the teams trot back with the limbers to the rear,
leaving the guns to be worked by the gunners.
At the same time the signal is sent back to
the waggons, who, meanwhile, have been halted
in the rear, if possible under cover, to send up
two waggons. Two are told off, and they trot
up to the firing line. 'Halt,' 'Unhook!' The
wheelers are rapidly unhooked, the team trots
back again to the rear. Presently two more are
called up with more ammunition. These do the
same thing, but after unhooking trot round and
hook into the other two (now empty) waggons,
and trot them back. The empty waggons are
refilled from the mule-waggons, which follow the
battery with the reserve shells, and their black
crews and all. 'Limber-supply,' that is, use of
the shells in the *gun*-limber, is only ordered in
the last resort or in exceptional cases. Finally,
when the firing position is to be changed,
the gun-limbers trot up; 'Limber up' is
given. The gun is hooked to the limber, and
the re-united machines trot away to the new

position, followed by the waggons. In some cases, too, when the waggons come up to the firing-line, they only leave the waggon-body there, trot away with the limber, and come back and 'limber up' later, in the same way as the gun. It all depends on how much ammunition is wanted. Of course, there are many variations of movement, but this is an average specimen.

"*June* 10.—*Sunday.*—I and Williams are stablemen, and the rest have gone to church parade. We have just had an icy wash with far-fetched water in an old ammunition box. The weather has turned very cold again at nights, with considerable frost. I have been sleeping out again though since the first week of our coming here, finding snug lairs under the quartermaster's stores. We have marching order parades most days now, and are pretty hard-worked. Yesterday we were reviewed by General Kelly-Kenny, together with another field-battery and a pom-pom battery. We trotted about in various formations, and the guns went into action once; and that was all. Our guns got into action

quicker than either of the regular batteries.
A message was communicated to us by the
General from Lord Roberts, saying we must not
be disappointed at not having gone to the front;
that there was plenty more work to be done, and
that meanwhile we were doing very useful work
in helping to guard this place. I am afraid we
are not very sanguine, but we never entirely lose
hope, and a wild idea that this review and the
other day's inspection might be preliminary to
an order to go up, cheered us up a lot for the time.
Camp rumours, too, are just as prolific and as
easily swallowed as before. Latterly there have
been all sorts of mysterious reports about the
Boers having got behind Roberts, re-taken
Kroonstadt and cut the railway, massacring
various regiments, whose names change hourly.
A camp rumour is a wonderful thing. Generally
speaking, there are two varieties, cook-shop
rumours and officers' servants' rumours. Both
are always false, but there is a slightly more
respectable mendacity about the latter than
the former. The cooks are always supposed

to know if we are changing camp by getting
orders about rations in advance. Having this
slight advantage, they go out of their way
to make rumours on every sort of subject.
How many scores of times the cooks have
sent us to the front I shouldn't like to say.
Officers' servants of course pick up scraps of in-
formation from their masters' tents ; in the pro-
cess of transmission to the battery at large the
original gets wide variations. We are often just
like kitchenmaids and footmen discussing their
betters. You will hear heated arguments going
on as to the meaning of some overheard remarks,
and the odd thing is that it no longer seems
strange.

" *June* 13.— . . . The moon was full this day,
and to see it rising sheer out of the level veldt
was a thing to remember. For ten minutes before
there is a red glow on the horizon, which intensi-
fies till a burning orange rim shows above, and
soon the whole circle is flaming clear of the
earth, only not a circle, but seemingly almost
square with rounded corners. Round its path

on the veldt there is a broad wash of dusty gold.
A lot of us came out of the tents, and were spell-
bound by the sight. Every evening the sun
goes down plumb into the veldt out of a cloudless sky, and comes up just so in the morning.
While he is gone it is bitterly cold now, always
with hard frost, but in the middle of the day
often very hot. I have never known such
extremes of temperature before.

"*June* 16.—Yesterday was a red-letter day
for me and Williams. We got leave off afternoon
stables, getting gunners to water and groom our
horses, and had from after dinner till 8.30 P.M.
to ourselves. That was the first time I have
ever missed duty from any cause whatever since
I enlisted on January 3rd, so I think I deserved
it. We started off, feeling strangely free, and
hardly knowing how to use our freedom, for
two hours is the longest interval from work one
usually gets. We determined to visit the Irish
Hospital Camp, where four of our chaps were
sick. The Irish Hospital came out with us in
the *Montfort*, so we knew them all. We hired

a carriage in the town (!) and drove the rest
of the way feeling like lords. We had a long
talk with the invalids, who were mostly doing
well, in most comfortable quarters, large roomy
tents, with comfortable beds, and clean white
nurses going about. Pat Duffy turned up as a
hospital orderly, looking strangely clean. The
air was heavy with rich brogue. Later we
strolled off, and shopped and shaved in the town,
had afternoon tea, and then went to a hotel and
wrote letters till 6.30, when we dined in magnificent style, and then sauntered back, feeling as
if an eternity had passed, and lay down in the
dust to sleep.

"*June* 17.—*Sunday.*—A night and day of
rain, in spite of the fact that everybody was
clear hitherto that the rainy season was over
months ago. Exercise at eight, and a smart trot
round the country warmed horses and men, for
it is very cold. Meanwhile, the horse lines
had been shifted, for they were ankle-deep in
mud. Once or twice in the day we were called
out to rub legs, ears, and backs of the horses.

"I am now lying on my back in our tent on a carefully constructed couch of sacks, rugs, and haversacks, with a candle stuck in a Worcester sauce bottle to light me. Most of us are doing the same, so the view is that of the soles of muddy boots against strong light, the tentpole in the middle hung thick with water-bottles, helmets, and haversacks, spurs strung up round the brailing, faces (dirty) seen dimly in the gloom beneath. Some write, some sew, some read. One is muttering maledictions over a tin of treacle he has spilt on his bed (he thought it was empty and stuck a candle on the bottom); one is telling stories (which nobody listens to) of happy sprees in far-off London. The air is thick with tobacco-smoke. Outside there is a murmur of stablemen trying to fit shrunk nose-bags on to restive horses, varied by the squeal and thump of an Argentine, as he gets home in the ribs of a neighbour who has been fed before him."

On the day after this was written our long period of waiting came to an end with orders to go at once to Kroonstadt.

G

CHAPTER V.

LINDLEY.

WE were off for the front at last, and I shall now, making a few necessary alterations, transcribe my diary, as I wrote it from day to day and often hour to hour, under all sorts of varying conditions.

June 21.—7 A.M.—I am writing this on the seat of a gun in an open truck on the way by rail to Kroonstadt. I have been trying to sleep on the floor, but it wasn't a success, owing to frozen feet. Now the sun is up and banishing the hoar-frost from the veldt, and the great lonely pasture-plain we are travelling slowly through looks wonderfully pleasant.

But I must go back.

Yesterday afternoon things looked profoundly settled. I walked down to town with a lot of clothes, and left them to be washed by a nigger, and also left my watch to be mended. But when I got back to "stables" it was announced that we were to leave for Kroonstadt that night. There was great joy, though I fear it means nothing. It's true De Wet and some rebels have been giving trouble round there, and even held up a train, and captured a battalion of militia not long ago; but I believe it's all over now. It was soon dark, and camp had to be struck and horses harnessed in the dark. I got leave, ran down to town and fetched up my unwashed clothes, and put most of them on there and then. There was the usual busy scene of packing kit, striking tents, drawing rations, filling water-bottles; the whole scene lit up by blazing bon-fires of rubbish. In leaving a camp no litter may be left; it has to be left as clean as the surrounding veldt. At nine hot coffee was served out, and at 9.45 "boot and saddle" went. Harnessing in pitch dark is not very easy, unless you have everything exactly where you can lay your hand on it.

We marched down to the station, and unharnessed near the platform in a deposit of thick
mud.   Entraining lasted all night, the mules
and buck-waggons giving a lot of trouble.   Some
exciting loose-mule-hunts round the station in
the dark.   Hours of shoving, hauling, lifting,
slamming.   At last all was in but ourselves.
There were evidently no carriages, so we
hurriedly shovelled our kit and ourselves into
the open gun-trucks, squirming into cracks and
corners ; and at 6.30 A.M. to-day, with the sun
just topping the distant veldt, the whistle blew,
and we started.   It was a piercing frosty morning ; but we were all so tired that we slept just
as we were.   I found myself nestling on the
floor of a truck (very dirty), between a gun-
wheel and the three foot high side with feed-
bags for pillows.   Cold feet soon roused me, and
I got up on to the gun in the sun, and saw we
were slowly climbing a long incline through the
usual veldt and kopjes, only more inhabited
looking, with a tree and a farm or two.   A lovely
scene with the sun reddening the veldt in the

pure crisp air. I smoked a cigarette in great content of mind. Soon shapeless heaps of blankets began to move down the trucks, muffled heads blinked out from odd corners, and gradually the Battery woke, and thawed, and breakfasted on biscuit and bully beef.. We have said good-bye to bread.

We rumbled slowly on all the morning, past the same sort of country, with dead horses and broken bridges marking Roberts's track, and at Brandfort stopped to feed horses, which, by the way, is a nasty dangerous game when you are dealing with closed horse-boxes. You have to climb through a small window, get in among the horses, and put the feeds on as they are handed up. The horses are not tied up, and are wild with hunger. You have simply to fight to avoid being crushed or kicked in that reeking interior, for they are packed as thick as possible.

At Vet River we got the first news of fighting. Boers under De Wet had been breaking bridges, and cutting wires. A very seedy-looking

Guardsman gave us the news, and said they were cold and starving; and they looked it. What regiment was there? "Oh, we're all details 'ere," he said, with a gloomy shrug. At Zand River infantry were in trenches expecting attack. A fine bridge had been blown up, and we crossed the river, which runs in a deep ravine, by a temporary bridge built low down, the track to it most ingeniously engineered in a spiral way. An engineer told us they had had hard fighting there a day or two ago. We reached Kroonstadt about dark; but remained outside all night, supperless and freezing.

June 22.—I walked about most of the night, and got an engine driver to squirt some hot water into a mess-tin to make tea with out of tablets. In early morning a train disgorged a crowd of men who had been prisoners with the Boers at Pretoria, some ever since the first battle. When Roberts came they all escaped, under shell-fire from the Boers as a final *congé*. They were a most motley crew, dressed in all manner of odd clothes. At 7 P.M. coffee and porridge, and at 7.30 orders came to detrain and harness up sharp, the sections to separate again. Then followed a whole series of contrary orders, but we ultimately harnessed up and hooked in ; the right section marched away, and soon after we of the left section did so too, about two o'clock. About three miles off, after climbing a long hill, we unlimbered the guns in a commanding position, and remained there till dark, in the close and fragrant neighbourhood of about twenty dead horses. I believe we had something to do with some possible or probable fight, but what, I don't know. A very dull battle. We marched back at dark, and bivouacked near the town, close to some Lancers. Of course tents are said good-bye to now. I slept by my harness, very cold.

June 23.—I woke early and chatted to the Lancers' cook over a roaring wood fire till reveillé. Orders came to start at two, as part of the escort of a convoy going to Lindley, distant about fifty miles east. Something real to do at last. Quiet morning; sewed buttons

on. At one "boot and saddle," and at two we
started and joined the convoy, a long train of
ox-waggons, with some traction engines drawing trucks. Our officers are Captain Budworth
(in command) and Lieutenant Bayley, just as
at Piquetberg Road. The troops with us are
some Buffs Militia, Yorkshire Light Infantry,
Australian Mounted Infantry (Imperial Bushmen Contingent), and some Middlesex Yeomanry.
Went through the rambling white desolate town,
forded a broad river, mounted a steep hill, and
came out on the open, rolling veldt. Here
we halted till near sunset, waiting for some
waggons, and many and eager were our specula-
tions on what was in store for us on this first
step into the field of war. For the first time
we saw and talked to infantry on the march.
Our escort (there is always an escort for guns)
is a company of Buffs, lean, stained, ragged, and
very *blasé* about this journey which they have
made twice before. They are short of most
things, and pitifully clad. I saw two with
no breeches, only- under-pants. All say they

are " fed up," a phrase always used out here to
mean " sick and tired of the war." The Bushmen seem a pleasant set of fellows. It is their
first campaign too.

When the truant waggons came up we
marched on a few miles, following the road,
which is just a hard track across the veldt,
and bivouacked for the night, the out-spanned
waggons ranged in rows in a rough square, as
far as I could see, but it was very dark, and we
had plenty to do ourselves. After unhooking,
we drivers had a long ride over the veldt to a
watering-place, losing the way in the dark two
or three times. It was late when we got back
to camp, guided by the fires. We unharnessed,
fed the horses, swallowed some tea and biscuit,
and laid down as we were to sleep.

June 24—*Sunday.*—Up at 3.45 A.M. and
harnessed; very cold. We started at five, in the
dark, and marched over rolling switchback veldt
till 9.30, and then halted to let the convoy oxen
get their day's graze and chew. Unharnessed
our horses. Coffee and porridge. I went on

fatigue to fill water-bottles at a filthy pond, and afterwards laboriously filtered some in a rather useless filter, which is carried on the gun. The water was so foul that the filter had to be opened and cleaned every four strokes.

At 12.45 we harnessed up and started again. I am writing now at one of the periodical halts, when every one dismounts. A soft, mild sunset is laying changing tints of colour on the veldt, rose, amber, fawn, with deep blue shadows. When I speak of *veldt* I mean simply grass-land, but not a hint of green in it. The natural colour at this season is buff, with a warm red undertone. When the setting or rising sun catches this the effect is exquisite.

There is a rumour that a Boer patrol has been sighted, and a prisoner captured. I believe there is no doubt that De Wet and his force are between us and Lindley, and will have a shot at this convoy. We were warned that we might be attacked to-night. At dark we bivouacked, and, soon after, our right section, under the Major, whom we parted from at

Kroonstadt, marched in. They had been sent
out with a relief column to Honing Spruit,
where a train had been attacked and the
troops in it hard pressed. The Boers cleared
off just before the Battery came up, which
then had followed and overtaken us. Another
bothersome hunt after water for the horses in
the dark. All we could find was a stagnant
pool, which ought to poison those that drank
of it. Some more troops also joined the column.
Colonel Brookfield (M.P.) is in command of
the whole force.

June 25—(*My birthday*).—Up at 4.15 A.M.
Off at 5.15, as part of the advance guard of the
column, the Bushmen and Yeomanry scouting
far ahead, and the infantry on either flank in
a widely extended line. We all admired the
steady regularity of their marching, heavily
weighted as they were. Our own gunners also
have a good deal of walking to do. " Dismount
the detachment " is the order at all up-grades, and
at difficult bits of the road. Drivers dismount
at every halt, however short, but on the move

are always safe in the saddle. We marched
over the same undulating land, with occasional
drifts and *spruits*, which are very hard on the
horses. The convoy behind looked like a long
sinuous serpent. Watered at seven at a farm.
Williams was sent out to forage, and bought
a sheep for 15*s.*, chickens at 1*s.* 6*d.*, and a
turkey. Gunners were sent out to pillage a
maize field. Then we marched on some miles
to the top of a steep ridge looking down upon a
lower plain, the road crossing a deep ravine at
the bottom by a big steel bridge. We took up
a commanding position at the top, overlooking
the bridge, so as to cover the convoy while it
descended and crossed. An attack seems likely,
—a curious birthday treat !—4 P.M.—Nothing
has happened. An interminable procession of
ox and mule-waggons files down the pass; it
is a much larger convoy than I thought, and
must have received additions since we started.
At this rate we shall be ages getting to Lindley.

One no longer wonders at the slowness of an
army's movement out here. The standard of

speed is the trek-ox, lurching pensively along
under his yoke, very exacting about his meal-
times, and with no high notions about supreme
efforts, when he has to get his waggon out of a
bad drift. He often prefers to die, and while he
is making up his ponderous mind he may be
blocking up a column, miles in length, of other
waggons in single file. We talk of the superior
mobility of the Boers; but it puzzles me to
know how they got it, for oxen and mules are
their standards of speed too, I suppose.

At dark, when all had passed, we followed
ourselves down an abominably dangerous road,
and over the bridge to camp, which looked and
sounded like a big busy town, scintillating with
fires and resonant with the yells of black drivers
packing their waggons.

June 26—*Eight* A.M.—We are in action, my
waggon at present halted in the rear. We
harnessed up at 3.45 this morning, and marched
some miles to the top of another hill, overlooking another plain, a crescent of steep kopjes on
the left, occupied by Boers. The convoy halted

just as a spattering rifle-fire ahead struck on the
still morning air (it was just dawn), and the
chatter of a Maxim on the left flank. We were
all rather silent.   A staff-officer galloped up,
"Walk,—March," "Trot," rang out to the Battery, and we trotted ahead down the hill, plunged
down a villainous spruit, and came up on to the
level, under a pretty heavy fire from the kopje on
our left.   For my part, I was absorbed for these
moments in a threatened mishap to my harness,
and the dread of disgrace at such an epoch.   My
off horse had lost flesh in the last few days, and
the girth, though buckled up in the last hole,
was slightly too loose. We had to gallop up a
steep bit of ascent out of the drift, and to my
horror, the pack-saddle on him began to slip and
turn, so I had to go into action holding on his
saddle with my right hand, in a fever of anxiety,
and at first oblivious of anything else.   Then I
noticed the whing of bullets, and dust spots
knocked up, and felt the same sort of feeling
that one has while waiting to start for a race,
only with an added chill and thrill.

The guns unlimbered, and came into action against the kopje, and we and the limbers trotted about 300 yards back, and are waiting there now. A gunner and a driver slightly wounded, and some horses hit. One bullet broke our wheel-driver's whip. Our shrapnel are bursting beautifully over the Boer lines.

(*Later.*)—We have just taken our waggon up to the firing line, and brought back an empty one with our team.

(*Later.*)—We have been back to the convoy, and refilled the empty waggon from the reserve, and are back again. The Boers seem to be dislodged from the ridge, and infantry have occupied it. I hear some Boers made for a farm, but we plumped a shell right into it, and they fled. The convoy is now coming on, and crossing the drift with discordant yells. Infantry and mounted infantry pressing on both flanks. Our guns have taken up another position farther on. The Captain asked after the broken whip, and told us we could not have gone into action better. He has been riding about all day on his stumpy little Argentine, radiant and beaming, with his eternal pipe in his mouth!

(*Later.*)—We marched on a few miles, and bivouacked, while the whole convoy slowly trailed in, and formed up in laager. This operation, and the business of posting the troops for the night, is horribly tedious. It has to be done in the dark, and one is continually mounting and dismounting, and moving on a bit, and making impossible wheels round mules and waggons. Probably we get too small a space allotted, and the horses are all jammed together in the picket-lines, causing a vast loss of temper at unharnessing. After unharnessing and feeding horses, which you have to look sharp about, or you will miss coffee, every one crowds round the cook's fire, and looks with hungry eyes at the pots. Coffee or tea, biscuits and tinned meat, are served out. You are ravenous, as you have lived on chance scraps during the day. Then you make your bed, stretching your blankets behind your harness, standing a saddle on end, and putting a feed-bag

behind it for a pillow. Next morning's feeds
have first to be made up, and then you sleep
like a log, if you can, that is. I generally have
to get up at least once, and walk about for the
cold. Fellows who are lucky enough to have
fuel make small fires (an anthill provides a
natural stove), and cook soup, but it's hard to
spare the water, which is as precious as gold in
this country. Besides, drivers are badly placed
for such luxuries ; their work is only begun
when camp is reached, while gunners can go
off and find beds under waggons, etc. It is the
same all day, except, of course, in action, when
the gunners have all the work. At all halts we
have to be watching a pair of horses, which have
manifold ways of tormenting one. To begin
with, they are always hungry, because they get
little oats and no hay. One of mine amuses
himself by chewing all leather-work in his
reach, especially that on the traces, and has to
be incessantly worried out of it. The poor
brutes are standing all the time on rich pasture,
and try vainly to graze. They are not allowed

H

to, as it involves taking out big bits, undoing
wither straps, etc., and you have to be ready to
start at a moment's notice. There are thousands
of acres of rich pasture all about, vast un-
developed wealth. Farms are very few and far
between; mostly dismal-looking stone houses,
without a trace of garden or adornment of any
sort. There was a load off all our minds this
night, for the H.A.C. had at last been in action
and under fire. All went well and steadily.
My friend Ramsey, the lead-driver of our team,
brushed his teeth at the usual intervals. I
don't believe anything on earth would interfere
with him in this most admirable duty. He
does it with miraculous dexterity and rapidity
at the oddest moments, saying it rests him !

June 27.—Up at 3.45 and harnessed, but it
was almost dawn before our unwieldy convoy
creaked and groaned into motion. We are rear-
guard to-day, with some Yeomanry, Australians,
and Buffs, but just now we were ordered up to
the front, trotted past the whole convoy, and
are now in action; limbers and waggons halted

behind a rise. The Boers have guns in action
to-day, and a shell of theirs has just burst about
400 yards to our right, and others are falling
somewhere near the guns ahead. It seems to
be chiefly an artillery duel so far, but a crackling
rifle fire is going on in the distance.

(*Midday.*)—The convoy is closing up and
getting into a sort of square. We have changed
positions several times. Shells have fallen pretty
close, but have done no damage. Some of them
burst, others only raise a cloud of dust. We
are already getting used to them, but the first
that fell made us all very silent, and me, at any
rate, very uncomfortable. Later we relieved
ourselves by a rather overstrained interest in
their probable direction and point of impact.
We were standing waiting, of course, with no
excitement to distract our minds.

(2 P.M.)—A curious feature in the scene is
the presence of veldt fires all over the place,
long lines of dry grass blazing. Possibly the
Boers start them to hide their movements. The
Boers evidently want this convoy; they are

right round our rear and on both flanks; all our troops are engaged. The convoy is being moved on, and my section is left as rear-guard. The smoke of burning grass has blotted out the sun, and it is cold. The sun is a red ball, as on a foggy day in London. Shells have ceased .to fall here, but a hill on the left is being heavily shelled by the enemy, and the infantry on it are in retreat.

(4 P.M.)—We are slowly getting on, covering the convoy's rear, the enemy pressing hard. Our guns are now firing over our dismounted troops. Williams has just ridden up. He has been orderly to the Captain; a shell fell just by his horse without bursting. I have been fearfully sleepy, and have snatched a few minutes of oblivion, during halts, on the ground by my horses, who are as tired as I am, poor beasts.

(*Written later.*)—The Boers, as it seemed to me (but what does one know?), had us in a very tight place, but they never pressed home their attack, and the convoy was rushed through the remaining seven miles to Lindley. We covered

its retirement till dark, and then followed it
with all speed. I shan't forget those seven
miles. They included the worst drifts of the
whole journey, and getting up and down them
in pitch-dark was unpleasant work and a pretty
severe test of driving. Three mule-waggons of
the convoy had to be abandoned at one place,
but the rest of it reached Lindley safely, as
did we. It was rather like making a port
after a storm when the lights appeared and a
bugle blowing "first post" was heard. We
passed some silent houses, groped into an open
space, picketed horses, chucked off harness, and
slept by it, dog-tired. We had hoped for a
good night's rest, but, the last thing, orders
went round for reveillé at four.

June 28.—It was icy cold at 4 A.M., and one's
fingers could hardly cope with straps and links.
I had done one horse, when welcome orders came
that my waggon was not wanted. So I sat by
the cook's fire and cooked in the lid of my mess-
tin a slice of meat I had hastily hacked from an
ox's carcase at our last camp. Also some Maggi

soup.   About sunrise the limbers returned,
having left the guns and gunners in position
on a hill somewhere, where they shot at any
Boers they saw, and were sniped at themselves.
A slack day for the rest of us, and I had a good
sleep.   Of course we are all delighted that the
days of waiting are over, and that we have had
fighting and been of use.   Everything has gone
well, and without a single hitch, and we were
congratulated by the Brigadier.   As for De
Wet, the plucky Boer who is fighting down here,
now that his cause is hopeless, we have sworn
to get him to London and give him a dinner
and a testimonial for giving us the chance of a
fight.

Of course the whole affair was trivial enough,
and I don't suppose will ever figure in the
papers, though it was interesting enough to us.
I should be sorry to have to describe what went
on as a whole.   I just wrote what was under my
eye during halts, and to grasp the plan of the
thing, when distances are so great and the enemy
so invisible, is impossible.   But, as far as I could

see, it was pretty well managed. We had no
casualties yesterday, chiefly owing to shells not
bursting. The Infantry and Yeomanry had
some killed and wounded, but I don't know the
numbers. Some of the Boer practice was excellent. Once we watched them shell some
Infantry on a kopje, every shell falling clean
and true on the top and reverse edge of it. The
Infantry had to quit. But on the whole I was
at a loss to understand their artillery tactics,
which seemed desultory and irresolute. They
would get our range or that of the convoy and
then cease firing, never concentrating their fire
on a definite point. Their ammunition too was
evidently of an inferior quality. I saw no
shrapnel fired. It is all very novel, laborious,
exciting, hungry work, and perhaps the strangest
sensation of all is one's passive ignorance of all
that is happening beyond one's own narrow
sphere of duty. An odd discovery is that one
has so much leisure, as a driver, when in action.
There is plenty of time to write one's diary when
waiting with the teams. One pleasant thing is

the change felt in the relaxation of the hard-and-fast regulations of a standing camp. Anything savouring of show or ceremonial, all needless *minutiæ* of routine, disappear naturally. It is business now, and everything is judged by the standard of common-sense.

The change of life since we left Bloemfontein has been complete ; no tents, no washing, no undressing, only biscuit and tinned-meat for food, and not too much of that, very little sleep, etc. ; but we have all enjoyed it, for it is the real thing at last. The lack of water was the only really trying thing, and the cold at night. We had fresh meat for supper this night from a sheep commandeered on the march, and weren't we ravenous ! Another very cold night, but the joyful orders for reveillé at 7 A.M.

June 29.—" Stables " and harness-cleaning all the morning. In the afternoon we were sent to graze our horses outside the town with a warning to look out for sniping. As I write I am sitting under a rock, the reins secured to one of my legs, which accounts for bad writing.

Lindley is below, a mere little village with a few
stores, which nevertheless was for a proud week
the capital of the Free State. For some time
past it has been closely besieged by the Boers,
and entirely dependent on one or two armed
convoys like ours. The Boers have been shelling
the town most days, and fighting goes on outside nearly every day. The day before we
relieved it the Boers made an effort to take it,
and our Infantry lost heavily. There was a
garrison of about a thousand, I think, before
we came. There is nothing eatable to be bought
at any price, and no communication with the
outside world, except by despatch-riders. I was
talking yesterday to two Yeomanry fellows who
had escaped from one of the Boer commandos.
They had lived entirely on fresh meat, and were
devouring dog-biscuit by our cook's fire like
famished terriers. They said they had been well
treated.

June 30.—Not much rest was allowed us.
Reveillé was at 4 A.M., with orders for our section, under Lieutenant Bayley, to march half-way

to Kroonstadt again, as part of an escort for a return convoy carrying sick and wounded.

Started at five with Yeomanry, Bushmen, and Buffs, as before, but were delayed two hours outside town, waiting for some traction engines, which puffed asthmatically at the bottom of a drift, unable to get up. Marched rapidly for sixteen miles (most of the country burnt by veldt fires), over the same difficult road, and (for a luxury) encamped while it was still light. Washed in a river with great zest. Fresh mutton for supper. Turned in with orders for reveillé at 4 A.M. But at 11.30 P.M. we were all awakened by "Come on, get up and harness up." "Why, what's the time?" "11.30." However, up we got, not knowing why, tossed on harness, and started straight away back for Lindley, supposing they were being attacked. It was a hard march over those detestable drifts, in pitch dark and freezing cold, with one halt only of ten minutes. The centre driver has a trying time in bad places of the road, for at steep bits on the down grade, if the wheelers

get at all out of control, he has the pole bearing
down on him, either punching his horses and
making them kick, or probing for vulnerable
places in his own person. He has the responsibility of keeping his traces just so that they are
not slack, and yet that the horses are not in
draught and pulling the gun or waggon down.
The lead-driver has to pick the road and, with
one eye on the gun just ahead, to judge a pace
which will suit the wheel-driver, who at such
moments must have a fairly free hand. All
three live always in a fierce glare of criticism
from the gunners riding behind, who in their
nasty moments are apt to draw abusive com-
parisons between the relative dangers of shell-
fire and riding on a waggon. By the way, there
is always a healthy antagonism between gunners
and drivers. When one class speaks of the
other there is generally an adjective prefixed.

July 1.—*Sunday.*—We marched 'into camp
before dawn blear-eyed and hungry, to find
to our disgust that there was no hurry after all.
It seems an order had been received for the

whole Battery to march away this morning, to
join some column or other, so they sent a messenger to recall us. Meanwhile a countermanding order came to "Stand fast." So here
I am, at 8 A.M., sitting against my harness
in the blessed sunlight, warm, fed, sleepy, and
rather irritated. What is going to happen I
don't know. It's no use writing the rumours.

(*Later.*)—A sudden order to harness up. Did
so, and were all ready, when we were told to
take it off again. It seems General Clements
has come up near here with a division, and they
want to finish off De Wet at once. A quiet day.
I foraged in the town in the afternoon, but got
nothing, though I heard of mealy biscuits at
one cottage.

Later on we found a cottage kept by an
Englishwoman, who gave us delicious tea at 6*d.*
a cup, and again in the evening porridge at 6*d.*
a plate. There was a number of mixed soldiers
in there, all packed round the room, which was
dark and smoky, and full also of squalling
children. The way she kept her temper and

fed us was wonderful. It is safe to say that
nowadays one can always eat any amount at any
time of day. The service biscuit is the best of
its kind, I daresay, but not very satisfying, and
meat is not plentiful. We have never yet been
on full rations. Four is the full number of
biscuits. We generally get three. Sometimes
the meat-ration is a "Maconochie," which is a
tin of preserved meat and vegetables of a very
juicy and fatty nature, most fascinating when
you first know it, but apt to grow tinny and
chemical to the palate.

CHAPTER VI.

BETHLEHEM.

July 2.—Reveillé 5 A.M. Harnessed up, and afterwards marched out and joined a column of troops under General Paget. We have with us some Yorkshire Light Infantry, Munster Fusiliers, Yeomanry, Bushmen, and the 38th Field Battery. Where we are going we don't know, but I suppose after De Wet.*

* [Without knowing it at the time, we were joining in General Hunter's big enveloping movement, by which all the scattered commandos in this part of the Free State were to be driven into the mountains on the Basuto border and there surrounded. Paget's brigade (the 20th) was part of the cordon, which was gradually drawn closer by the concentric marches of columns under him, and General Clements, Rundle, Boyes, Bruce Hamilton, and Hunter himself. The climax was the surrender of about 5000 Boers under Prinsloo at Fouriesberg on July 29, a success much impaired by the escape of De Wet from the fast-closing trap. For the sake of clearness I append this note; but I leave my diary as I wrote it, when our knowledge of events rarely went beyond a foggy speculation.]

(8.30 A.M.)—We have marched for about two hours to the top of a range of hills which surrounds the town ; there is firing on the right and left, and the Infantry are advancing in extended order. Our right section has just gone into action. A big drove of wild-looking Boer ponies has come stampeding up to the column with some of our mounted men vainly trying to corner them.

(1.30 P.M.)—The battle is, as usual, unintelligible to the humble unit, but the force is advancing slowly, the Yorkshire Light Infantry and Munster Fusiliers on either hand of us. Our section is in action now. We have just taken our waggon to the firing line and brought back the team. The corporal's horse stepped in a hole just as we were reaching the guns and turned a complete somersault. He is all right, but his was our second mishap, as' the near wheeler fell earlier in the day, and the driver was dragged some yards before we could stop. The ground is very dangerous, full of holes, some of them deep and half-covered

with grass. Another driver is up, but the
former is only a bit shaken, I think. Our
section has silenced a Boer gun in three shots,
at 4200 yards, a good bit of work, and a credit
to Lieutenant Bayley as a judge of range. The
right section also cleared the kopje they fired at,
but had a narrow escape afterwards, coming
suddenly, when on the move, under the fire of
Boer guns, of whose presence they were ignorant,
the shells falling thick but not bursting.
Bivouacked at four on the veldt. The Boers had
retired from the line they held. A long ride to
water after unharnessing; nothing much to eat.
Williams and I have taken to ending the
day by boiling tea (from tablets) over the
embers of the cook's fire, or on one of our
own if we have any fuel, which is very
seldom. How the cooks get their wood is
a mystery to me. The Kaffir drivers always
have it, too, though there are no visible trees.
We always seem to sit up late, short though
our nights are. A chilly little group gathers
sleepily round the embers, watching mess-tins

full of nondescript concoctions balanced cun-
ningly in the hot corners, and gossiping of
small camp affairs or large strategical movements of which we know nothing. The brigade
camp-fires twinkle faintly through the gloom.
A line of veldt-fire is sure to be glowing in the
distance, looking like the lights of a sea-side
town as seen from the sea. The only sound is
of mules shuffling aud jingling round the
waggons.

The "cook-house" is still the source of
rumours, which are wonderfully varied. There
is much vague talk now of General Clements
and a brigade being connected somehow with
our operations. But we know as little of the
game we are playing as pawns on the chess-
board. Our tea is strong, milkless, and sugar-
less, but I always go to sleep the instant I lie
down, even if I am restless with the cold later.

July 3.—Reveillé at 4.30. Our section, under
Lieutenant Bayley, started at once for a steep
kopje looming dimly about three miles away.
The right section, with the Major and Captain,

I

left us and went to another one. We had a tough job getting our guns and waggons up.

(8 A.M.)—Just opening fire now. A Boer gun is searching the valley on our left, but they can't see the limbers and waggons.

(8.30.)—The Boers seem to have some special dislike to our waggon. They have just placed two shells, one fifty yards in front of it, and the other fifty yards behind ; one of them burst on impact, the other didn't. The progress of a shell sounds far off like the hum of a mosquito, rising as it nears to a hoarse screech, and then "plump." We mind them very little now. There is great competition for the fragments, as "curios." It is cold, grey, and sunless to-day. Last night there was heavy rain, and our blankets are wet still. It seems the Boers are firing a Krupp at 7000 yards ; our guns are only sighted up to 5000 yards, but we have managed to reach them by sinking the trail in the ground, and other devices.

(12.30 P.M.)—A long halt here, with nothing doing. The Boer gun has ceased to fire, and we call it " silenced," possibly with truth, but the causes of silence are never quite certain. As far as I can make out, it was on the extreme left of their position, while our main attack is threatening their centre. It is raining hard, but we have made a roaring fire of what is the chief fuel in this country, dry cow-dung, and have made cocoa in our mess-tins, from a tin sent me a month ago; also soup, out of the scrapings of Maconochie tins.

——. What seemed likely to be a dull day turned out very exciting. About two a staff officer came up with orders, and we marched down from our kopje and attacked another one * (which I made out to be their centre), taking up several positions in quick succession. The Boers had a gun on the kopje, which we dislodged, and the infantry took the position. (About 2.30 it began to rain again and poured all the afternoon in cold, slashing torrents.) We finally went up the kopje ourselves, over a shocking bit

* The name of this kopje was Barking Kop, I believe, and we have since always applied it generally to the fighting on this day.

of rocky ground near the top, fired on the
retreating Boers from there, and then came
down on the other side.   Soon afterwards came
an old story.   It was about five, and had cleared
up.   A staff officer had said that there were no
Boers anywhere near now, and that we were to
march on and bivouac.   We and the Munsters and
some Yeomanry were marching down a valley,
whose flanks were supposed to have been scouted,
the infantry in column of companies, that is, in
close formation, and all in apparent security.
Suddenly a storm of rifle-fire broke out from a
ridge on our right front and showed us we were
ambushed.   The Munsters were nearest to
the ridge, about 600 yards, I should say.   We
were a bit further off.   I heard a sort of hoarse
murmur go up from the close mass of infantry,
and saw it boil, so to speak, and spread out.
Our section checked for a moment, in a sort of
bewilderment (my waggon was close behind our
gun at the time), but the next, and almost without orders, guns were unlimbered and whisked
round, a waggon unhooked, teams trotting away,

and shrapnel bursting over the top of the ridge
in quick succession. All this time the air was
full of a sound like the moaning of wind from
the bullets flying across the valley, but strange
to say, not a man of us was hit. Some of
them were explosive bullets. The whole thing
was soon over. Our guns peppered their
quickest, and it was a treat to see the shrapnel
bursting clean and true along the ridge. The
infantry extended and lay down; some Yeomanry
made a flank move, and that episode was over.
It might have been serious, though. If they had
held their fire undiscovered for ten minutes
longer we might have been badly cut up, for we
were steadily nearing the spur which they
occupied. It is right to say, though, that
our Lieutenant, having doubts about the
safety of the place, had shortly before sent
forward ground-scouts, of whom Williams was
one, who would possibly have been able to warn
us in time. Needless to say, it was not our duty
to scout for the column.

It was nearly dark now, a burning farm ahead

making a hot glow in the sky, and we moved off
to join the rest of the column with its unwieldy
baggage-train and convoy, and all camped together, after the usual tedious ride to water
horses at a muddy pool. They had had a very
hard day and had done well, but were very
tired. On days like this they often get no
water till evening. A feed is ordered when a
free interval seems likely, but the chances are that
it is snatched off, and their bits thrust in again,
half-way through. When we got in and rejoined
our right section, all were full of a serious mishap
to the 38th Field Battery, with which they had
been acting on the left flank. Both were in
action in adjoining fields, when a party of Boers
crept up unseen and got within fifty yards of
the 38th guns, shooting down men and horses.
The 38th behaved splendidly, but all their
officers were killed or wounded, a number of
gunners, and many horses. Two guns were
for a time in the hands of the Boers, who, I
believe, removed the tangent sights. It appears
that the M.I. escort of the Battery, owing, I

suppose, to some misunderstanding, retreated.
The situation was saved by Captain Budworth,
of our Battery, who collected and brought up
some mounted infantry, whether Yeomanry or
Bushmen I am not clear about. They beat the
Boers off, and our teams helped to take the guns
out of action. We came off all right, with only
one gunner slightly wounded.

I was desperately hungry, and only coffee was
issued, but later a sheep's carcase turned up from
somewhere, and I secured a leg, and Williams
some chops, which we promptly laid as they were
on one of the niggers' wood fires and ate in our
fingers ravenously. The leg I also cooked and
kept for to-day (I am writing on the morning
of the 4th), and it is hanging on my saddle. I
was rather sleepless last night, owing to cramp
from a drenched blanket, and got up about midnight and walked over to the remains of one of
our niggers' fires. Crouching over the embers I
found a bearded figure, which hoarsely denounced
me for coming to its fire. I explained that it was
our fire, but that he was welcome, and settled

down to thaw. It turned out to be a sergeant
of the 38th Battery. I asked something, and
he began a long rambling soliloquy about things
in general, in a thick voice, with his beard
almost in the fire, scarcely aware of my presence.
I can't reproduce it faithfully, because of the
language, but it dealt with the war, which he
thought would end next February, and the
difference between Boer and British methods,
and how our cavalry go along, heels down,
toes in, arms close to side, eyes front, all according to regulation, keeping distance regardless of ground, while the Boer cares nothing as
long as he gets there and does his work. He
finished with the gloomy prophecy that if we
didn't join Clements to-morrow we should never
" get out of this." Not knowing who or where
Clements was, I asked him about the affair of that
day, and produced a growling storm of expletives ;
then he muttered something about the Victoria
Cross and driving a team out of action, asked the
way to his lines, to which I carefully directed
him, and drifted off in the opposite direction.

By the way, this General Clements seems to be a myth, and the talk now is of Rundle and Ian Hamilton, who are supposed to be getting round De Wet from other quarters, while we drive him up this way into their arms. It is said we are going to Bethlehem. I forgot an important event of the evening in the arrival of a bag of mails, parcels only, brought by a convoy from Kroonstadt, which has just come in. To my delight I got one with a shirt and socks (which I at once put on over the others), cigarettes (a long exhausted luxury), Liebig, precious for evening soup, and chocolate, almost too good to eat for fear of getting discontented. We are on half rations of biscuit, which means three, and a tin of Maconochie each, a supply about enough to whet your appetite for one meal in a life like this, but it has to last the day of about seventeen hours. The ration is issued the night before, to eat as we please, and, of course, there is coffee soon after reveillé, and tea in the evening. There is a cupful of porridge also with the coffee, paid for by deduction from our pay, so that one starts in good fettle. I don't know why the whole column shouldn't get fresh meat every day, for the country is teeming with cattle, which are collected and driven along with the column in huge herds. Many of the farmhouses are smoking ruins, the enemy, after annexation, being rebels according to law, and not belligerents; but it seems to me that such a policy is to use a legal fiction for an oppressive end, for it is quite clear that this part of the Orange River Colony has never been conquered.*

July 4.—*Wednesday.*—Up at five after a bitterly cold night, but there was a long delay before starting. We are rear-guard to-day. Just before leaving an infantry man shot himself while cleaning his rifle. There was a little buzz and stir, and then all was quiet again. He was buried in half an hour.

A dull day's marching. After about ten

---

* I leave this as I wrote it, but drivers are not politicians, and doubtless there were special circumstances, such as treachery, concealed arms or sniping, to justify what at the best must be a doubtful policy; for a burnt farm means a desperate farmer.

miles we halted to water horses and rest. While
watering, the Boers sent over a futile shell from
a big gun. On return we unhooked and grazed
the horses. Things looked peaceful, and there
was a warm sun, so I ventured to unstrap my
kit-roll and spread my blankets out to dry.
They were still wet from the rain of two nights
ago. I had scarcely spread them out when
" Hook in " was shouted, and back they had to
go, half-folded, in a perilously loose bundle.
(You can never count on five minutes, but it's
worth trying.) At about 4.30 we and the 38th
Battery trotted ahead about a mile and a half,
and began shelling a ridge ; but I think it was
soon abandoned, for shortly after we limbered up
and camped with the rest of the brigade, which
had followed us. I am " stableman " to-day for
three days. On the march this involves drawing
sacks of forage from the Quartermaster Sergeant
in the early morning and late evening, and serving
out the oats to the drivers of the sub-division. It
is not so irksome a duty as in a standing camp,
but has its trying moments ; for instance, when

drivers are busied with bed-making or cocoa-
cooking in the evening, and are deaf to your
shouts of " D drivers, roll up for your feeds ! " a
camp-cry which has not half the effect of " Roll
up for your coffee ! " or, more electrical still,
" Roll up for your rum ! "

July 5.—We were up at 4.30, but as usual
had to stand by our horses for over an hour,
freezing our feet in the frosty grass before
starting. Harnessing up with numbed fingers
in the dark was a trying job. My harness sheets
were stiff as boards with frozen dew, and I
had to stamp them into shape for packing. I
had a warm night, though. My bed is made
thus : I place the two saddles on end, at the
right distance for the length of my body, and
facing inwards, that is, with the seats out-
wards; I leave the horse-blankets strapped
on underneath them, as there is not much time
to re-fold and re-strap them in the morning, and
my head (pillowed on two feed-bags filled overnight for the early morning feed) goes in the
hollow of one saddle, between the folds of

the blanket, and my feet in the hollow of the
other. The rest of each set of harness is heaped
behind each saddle, and when the harness-sheets
are spread over each set there is enough for the
ends to lap over and make a roof for the head,
and also for the feet. Then I wrap myself in
my two blankets, and if an oatsack is obtainable,
first get my feet into that. My waterproof
sheet serves as counterpane. It is not wanted
as a mattress, as no dew falls till the morning,
and the ground is dry at bed-time. After rain,
of course, it has to go beneath one. The great
point is to keep your blankets as dry as you can,
for, once wet with dew or rain, they remain wet,
since we both start and arrive in the dark, and
thus cannot count on drying them. It is a good
plan before turning in to see that the horses in
the lines near you are securely tied up, as it is
vexatious to be walked on in the night by a
heavy artillery horse; also to have all your kit
and belongings exactly where you can lay hands
on them in the dark. At reveillé, which, by
the way, takes the shape of a rude shake

from the picket of the night (there is no
trumpet used in campaigning), you shiver out of
your nest, the Sergeant-Major's whistle blows,
and you at once feed your horses. Then you
pack your off-saddle, rolling the ground-sheet,
blankets, and harness-sheet, with the muzzles,
surcingle-pads, hay-nets, etc., and strapping the
roll on the saddle. Then you harness as fast as
you can (generally helped by a gunner), make
up two fresh feeds and tie them up in nose-bags
on the saddle, and put on your belt, haversack,
water-bottle, and other accoutrements. In the
middle of this there will be a cry of " D coffee
up!" and you drop everything and run with the
crowd for your life to get that precious fluid,
and the porridge, if there is any. You bolt
them in thirty seconds, and run back to strap
your mess-tin on your saddle, put the last
touches to your harness, and hook in the team.
Of course we sleep in our cloaks, and wear them
till about eight, when the sun gets strength.
Then we seize a chance to roll them at a halt,
and strap them in front of the riding saddle.

To return to to-day. It has been very in-conclusive and unsatisfactory. We have marched about twelve miles, I think, with some long halts, in one of which we unhooked and rode to a pool some distance off to water horses. I have been fearfully sleepy all day. Two guns of the 38th Battery have joined us, and we march as a six-gun battery under Major McMicking. They have no officers fit for duty, and our Captain looks after them. In the evening some shrapnel began bursting on a ridge ahead, and we went up and fired a bit; but I suppose the Boers decamped, for we soon after halted for the night. It is said that the mythical Clements is now one march behind us, our scouts having met to-day, and that Bethlehem is three miles ahead, strongly held by De Wet. Other mythical generals are in the air. I am getting used to the state of blank ignorance in which we live. Perfect sunset in a clear sky. One of the charms of Africa is the long settled periods of pure unclouded sky, in which the sun rises and sets with no flaming splashes of vivid

colours, but by gentle, imperceptible grada-
tions of pure light, waning or waxing. And as
for rain, when it is once over it is thoroughly
over (at this season, at any rate). This night
the darkness was soon lit up by a flaming farm.
All desperately hungry, when it was announced
that an extra ration of raw meat was to be
served out. If I can't cook it, shall I eat it
raw? To-morrow's ration is a pound of fresh
cooked meat, instead of the eternal Maconochie.
It was drawn to-night, and looked so good that
I ate half of it at once, thus yielding to an oft-
recurring temptation. Orders for reveillé at
seven. Great joy.

July 6.—Reveillé was marked by a Boer shell
coming over the camp, followed by others in
quick succession, real good bursting shrapnel, a
rare thing for the Boers to possess, but they
came from a long range and burst too high.
Nobody took the least notice, and we went
on harnessing and breakfasting as usual. It is
strange how soon one gets a contempt for shells.
In about half an hour the firing stopped. We

hooked in, but unhooked again, and rode to water. There is some delay; waiting for Clements, perhaps. I write this sitting by my horses in a hot sun, with the water frozen to a solid lump in the bottle at my back, through the felt cover, and after being under a harness sheet all the night. Had a jolly talk with some Paddies of the Munster Fusiliers, about Ireland, etc. They were miserable, "fed up," but merry; that strange combination one sees so much of out here. They talked about the revels they would have when they got home, the beef, bacon, and stout, but chiefly stout. We have already learnt to respect and admire the infantry of our brigade, and I think the confidence is mutual. (Starting.)

(4.30).—We have had a hard day's marching a long distance out on the right flank. There is a biggish battle proceeding.

I think Clements's brigade has joined ours, for our front is some miles in length, with the wavy lines of khaki figures advancing slowly and steadily, covered by artillery fire. The 38th are with us. We have been in action several

K

times in successive positions, but the chief
attack seems to be on a steep conical kopje in
the centre, behind and below which lies Bethlehem, I believe. It is just dark, but heavy
rifle-firing is still going on in front. One of our
gunners has been shot in the knee. We camped
near our last firing position, but waited a long
time for our transport and its precious freight of
cooks and " dickseys " (camp-kettles). Williams
and I ruthlessly chopped down parts of a very
good fence, and made a fire with the wood and
a lot of dry mealy stalks, which burn furiously.
Then we and Ramsey cooked our meat in our
mess-tin lids, and made cocoa with water which
Ramsey fetched from some distance. It was a
thick brown fluid, and froze while we were
waiting to put it on, but it tasted excellent.

July 7.—Reveillé at 3.45. We marched out
about a mile and waited for the dawn.

7 A.M —At first dawn firing began, and we
went into action at once, as did the whole line of
infantry. A tremendous fusillade of shells and
bullets is now being poured upon the position

in front, and chiefly on the central conical
kopje. My waggon is halted, waiting to go up.
The sun is just getting strength, warming
our numbed feet, and spiriting away the white
frost-mantle that the land always wears at
dawn.

(3 P.M.).—Guns, Maxims, and rifles hailed
lead into the Boer trenches for a long time, and
then the infantry seized them, and the Boers
retired. The practice of the 38th and our guns
seemed to me to be very good. We have
also a five-inch lyddite gun (Clements brought
it), which sent up huge clouds of brown dust
where the shell struck. We have now advanced
over very heavy ground to the late Boer position, halted, and ridden some way to water down
a precipitous slope, into a long, rocky hollow.
From this point the country seems to change
entirely to steep, rocky hills and hollows, rising
and increasing to the whole Drakensberg range,
which is blue and craggy on the sky-line.
They say the Boers have evacuated Bethlehem
with a baggage train three miles long. I don't

know why we are not following them up. Perhaps the mounted infantry are. Our horses are done up. It was cruel work spurring and lashing them over heavy ploughed land to-day.

July 8.—Rest at last. It is Sunday morning, and we are all lying or sitting about, bathed in warm sunshine, waiting for orders, but it seems we shan't move to-day. My blankets are all spread out, getting a much-wanted drying, but what I chiefly want is a wash. I have had three imperfect ones since leaving Bloemfontein and one shave, and my boots off for about ten minutes now and then.

(3 P.M.).—Nothing on to-day. I have had a wash in a thimbleful of water, and shaved, and feel another man. They gave us an hour of stables, but the horses certainly needed it, as they never get groomed now, and are a shaggy, scraggy-looking lot. I'm glad to say mine are quite free from galls and sore backs. As one never sees their backs by daylight, it is interesting to get a good look at them at last. They are very liable to sore backs (partly owing to the

weight of the military saddle), if there is any
carelessness in folding the blanket beneath the
saddle. It has been a real hot day, and yet
there was thick ice on the pool we watered at
this morning.

As to yesterday, it appears that De Wet and
his army effected a safe retreat, but our General
was pleased with the day's work, and congratulated us and the 38th. We put one Boer gun
at least completely out of action, and it was
captured by the infantry. The infantry lost
but few that day, but rather heavily the day
before, especially the Munsters. Paget is already
very popular with us. We trust his generalship
and we like the man, for he seems to be one of
us, a frank, simple soldier, who thinks of every
man in his brigade as a comrade. I understand
now what an enormous difference this makes to
men in the ranks. A chance word of praise
dropped in our hearing, a joking remark during
a hot fight (repeated affectionately over every
camp-fire at night), any little touch of nature
that obliterates rank, and makes man and

general "chums" for the moment; such trifles
have an effect on one's spirits which I could never
have believed possible, if I had not felt their
charm. I wonder if officers know it, but it takes
nothing for them to endear themselves to men.

It seems to be beyond doubt that our guns
are a success, but their special ammunition is a
source of great difficulty. We have stacks of it
at Bloemfontein, but cannot carry much about
with us, and of course the ammunition column
with its fifteen-pounder shells is of no use to us.
We have been short after every action, and have
to depend on precarious waggonfuls, coming
by convoy from somewhere on the railway.
They say General Hunter and a division is
concentrating here too, and a large force is
visible in the valley, marching up. They are
flooding us with fresh meat to-day, by way of
a change. It is said that Paget has ordered
a certain number of sheep and cattle to be
slaughtered daily for the brigade.

(*Later*).—I had scarcely written the above
lines when the order came to harness up at

once. We did so, and were soon off; the sections separated, ours making for a steep hill about three miles away, on which we were ordered to take post. It was an awkward climb in the gathering darkness, with drag-ropes on the upper wheels, when moving along a very steep slope. A final rush of frantic collar work, and we were on a flat plateau, where we unlimbered the guns, so as to command the valley, and camped near them. I was on picket duty this night, and quite enjoyed it, though I had one three-hour spell at a go. It was warmer than usual, with a bonnie moon in a clear sky, a dozen veldt-fires reddening in the distance, mysterious mists wreathing about the valley beneath, and the glowing embers of a good wood-fire on which to cook myself some Maggi soup.

CHAPTER VII.

BULTFONTEIN.

July 9.—A delicious, warm day. Reveillé at six. I am afraid it looks as if we were to be kept on this lonely hill-top for some time. It's true we deserve a rest, for we have been on the move for some time; but I would much prefer to march on and see the last of De Wet. After campaigning, the routine of a standing camp seems dull and irksome. We have just shifted our camp a few hundred yards, bringing it to the very brow of the hill, which drops straight down into the valley. In fact, it is below the brow, and the horses are on a most awkward slant. The Munsters are camped just above us. Below, and about two miles away, lies Bethlehem, with hills behind it, and the mountain range mistily seen behind all. Unlike Lindley, this is the first time Bethlehem has been occupied by the British. Williams has just come in from a foraging expedition he was sent on. He got mealy flour for the battery, and a chicken for ourselves, and had had cigarettes and marmalade with the Lifeguards, who, with the whole of Hunter's division, are camped near here. He also got some Kaffir bread from a kraal, a damp, heavy composition, which, however, is very good when fried in fat in thin slices. We ate our tea sitting on rocks overlooking the valley, and at dark a marvellous spectacle began for our entertainment, a sight which Crystal-Palace-goers would give half-a-crown for a front place to see. As I have said, all day long there are casual veldt-fires springing up in this country. Just now two or three began down in the valley, tracing fine golden lines in spirals and circles. The grass is short, so that there is no great blaze, but the effect is that of some great unseen hand writing cabalistic sentences (perhaps the "Mene, Mene" of De

Wet !), with a pen dipped in fire.   This night
there was scarcely a breath of wind to determine
the track of the fires, or quicken their speed,
and they wound and intersected at their own
caprice, describing fantastic arcs and curves from
which one could imagine pictures and letters.
The valley gradually became full of a dull, soft
glow, and overhung with red, murky smoke,
through which the moon shone down with the
strangest mingling of diverse lights.   Very
suddenly a faint breeze began to blow in from
the valley directly towards our camp.   At once
the aimless traceries of fine flame seemed to
concentrate into a long resolute line, and a wave
of fire, roaring as it approached, gained the foot
of the hill, and began to climb it towards us.
Watchful   eyes   had   been   on   the   lookout.
" Drivers, stand to your horses," was shouted.
" Out with your blankets, men," to our gunners
and the infantry behind, and in an instant the
chosen sons of Cork were bounding out of their
lines and down the hill, and belabouring the fire
with   blankets   and   ground-sheets   and   sacks.

They seemed to think it a fine joke, and raised a pæan of triumph when it was got under. " Wan more victory," I heard one say.

July 10.—Slack day, most of it spent in grazing the horses. For this duty each man takes four horses, so that only half of us need go ; but on the other hand, if you stay, you may come in for a " fatigue," which it requires some insight to predict. Beyond that, our whole energies were concentrated on cooking our meals, raw meat only being served out. Williams and I borrowed a camp-kettle from the Munsters, and cooked our mutton with a pumpkin which we had commandeered. The weather is a good deal warmer. We are camped near the scene of a hard stand made by the Boers, dotted with trenches and little heaps of cartridge-cases, and also unused cartridges. I found one complete packet sewn up in canvas roughly and numbered. In most cases they are Lee-Metfords, and not Mausers. The Boers have, of course, captured quantities of our rifles and ammunition in convoy " mishaps " of various dates. Spent the

evening in trying cooking experiments with
mealy flour and some Neave's Food, which one
of us had.   One longs for a change of diet from
biscuit and plain meat, which, without vegetables, never seem to satisfy.   Even salt has
been lacking till to-day, and porridge has ceased.
It was announced that a convoy was to leave
for Kroonstadt the same night, taking wounded
and mails, and I hurriedly wrote two notes.   I
am afraid we are here for some time.   I wish
I could hear from Henry.

July 11.—Reveillé at 6.30.   Stables, grazing,
exercise, and more stables, till 1.30, and grazing
again in the afternoon.   Sat up late at night
over embers of cook's fire, talking to a Munster
sergeant about the last two days' fighting and
other experiences of his.   They had thirty-two
casualties on the second day, including four
officers wounded.   All sorts of rumours to-day :
that we stop a month on this hill ; that we go
to Capetown on Friday ; that we march to
Harrismith and Durban in a few days, etc., etc.

July 12.—At breakfast, mealy porridge was

served out with the coffee. It is eatable, but not pleasant without sugar.

Williams and I got leave to spend the morning out, and walked to Bethlehem over the veldt. A rather nice little town, but all the stores shut, and looking like a dead place. It was full of troops. Some stores had sentries over them, for there had been a great deal of looting. We hammered at a store door, and at last a man came out and said he had nothing to sell. However, he gave us leave to look round, which we did with an exhaustive scrutiny which amused him. At first there seemed to be nothing but linseed meal and mouth-organs, but by ferreting round, climbing to shelves, and opening countless drawers, we discovered some mealy flour, and reproached him for his insincerity. He protested that it was all he had to live on, but at last consented to sell us some, and some mixed spices, the only other eatable he had, besides a knife and fork, braces and sponges. Then we tried another store. A crusty, suspicious old fellow let us grudgingly in locked the door, and made the same protests. We were just going when I descried some bottles on a distant shelf. He sourly brought them down. They were Mellin's Food for Infants, and we bought six at half a crown each ; also some mixed herbs, and essence of vanilla. Then we made a house-to-house visitation, but only got some milk from an Englishwoman, who was so full of stories of Boer rapacity that she forgot our wants, and stood, cup in hand, complaining about eight ponies they had taken, while we were deaf and thirsty. The whole town had an English appearance. They all abused De Wet. No fresh supplies had come in for nine months, and the whole place was stripped. On the whole, we thought we had done pretty well, as we had half a sack of things, and another one full of fuel laboriously collected on the way back.

Rumours in the town were rife. All agreed we could do nothing till a supply-convoy comes in, now expected from Kroonstadt. We are fifty-four miles, across mountains, from Harrismith on the east, and seventy or eighty from Kroonstadt on the west. All supplies from the latter must come by ox-waggons over dozens of bad drifts, with raiding Boers about, and it is easy to see how an army might be starved before it knew it. We are very short now, I believe. It seems De Wet is ten miles off in the mountains, being watched by Broadwood's cavalry, and as soon as we can move I expect we shall go for him. Grazing in the afternoon. Williams and I played picquet, lying by our horses. This is always rather a precarious amusement, as the horses have a way of starting off suddenly to seek " pastures new," and you look up and find them gone, and have to climb rocks and view them out. We tie them all four close together, but there is generally one predominant partner who personally conducts the rest. In the evening we baked cakes of our mealy flour, adding Mellin's Food, mixed herbs, vanilla, and fat, and fried it in a fatty dish. It was very good, and was followed by meat fried in mealy crumbs, and later on, some mealy porridge and Mellin mixed. We tried Mellin alone first, but it seemed thin. We read the directions carefully, and used the proportions laid down for infants *over* three months. I dare say it would have been all right had we been four months old, but being rather more mature, it seemed unsubstantial. Its main advantage is its sweetness. In this hungry life, one misses sugar more than anything.

July 13.—Reveillé 6.30, and grooming, while the infantry chaps sat up in their beds and watched us sarcastically. At nine, harness-cleaning for drivers, and grazing for gunners, but I have got a gunner who dislikes bare-back riding to do my harness while I graze. I am writing on the veldt; warm sunny day, pale blue sky—very pale.—Back to finish harness cleaning. We always "grouse" at this occupation, as I believe all drivers do on active service. We don't polish steel, but there is a wonderful lot of hard work in rubbing dubbin into all the leather. It is absolutely necessary to keep it supple, especially such parts as the collar, girths, stirrup-leathers, reins, etc. Grazing again all the afternoon. The horses have been on half rations of oats since we came here, so I suppose it is necessary. I was sitting writing by my horses, when a cart rattled by. Some one shouted, "Anything to sell?" It stopped, and there was a rush. In it was a farmer and a rascally old Yeomanry sergeant who had been buying bread for his men, and now sold us a loaf and a half for six shillings. There was no doubt about paying, and I got a third of one loaf, which we ate luxuriously in the evening. It was of mealy flour, and tasted velvety and delicious after eternal biscuit. We also organized a large bake of mealy cakes, which were a distressing failure, as the pan got red-hot. I am afraid food and eating have become very prominent in my diary. My only excuse is that they really are not disproportionately so, seeing their absorbing importance in the life of a soldier on active service, especially when he is far from a base and rations are short.

Some Boer tobacco was kindly sent to us by

L

the Major, and was very welcome, for 'baccy has been very scarce, and you see fellows picking the wet dottels out of the bottoms of their pipes and drying them in the sun for future use. Matches also are very precious; there are none to be got, and they are counted and cared for like sovereigns. The striking of a match is a public event, of which the striker gives previous notice in a loud voice. Pipes are filled, and every second in the life of the match is utilized.

July 14.—We came back to camp after the last spell to find that the gunners had shifted the lines to the bottom of the hill, on a dismal patch of burnt veldt. We dragged and carried our harness and kit down the rocks, and settled down again, after the usual fatigues connected with change of camp. Everybody very irritable, for this looked like a long stay, but after tea the word went round that we were off next day, to our great delight. We are sick of this place.

July 15.—We harnessed up at 6.30, and at

9.30 climbed to the top of the hill again, a hard
pull for the horses. Then marched off with an
escort of Highlanders, and halted on what it
seems is the Senekal road, near to the site of
our last camp after the battle. Here we joined
our own right section and a large convoy with
sick and wounded, besides the transport for our
own brigade, which had mustered there too.
They say we are going with the convoy to
Senekal, which is quite unexpected, and a
doubtful prospect. It seems to be taking us
away from De Wet, and promises only hard
marching and a dull time. We marched
about ten miles entirely over burnt veldt, a
most dismal country. There was a high cold
wind, which drove black dust over us till we
were all like Christy Minstrels. Camped at
five.

July 16.—Reveillé at six. There was a
deficiency in the meat ration, and at the
last moment a sheep's carcase for each sub-
division was thrown down to be divided. Ours
was hacked to bits pretty soon, but raw meat

on the march is a great nuisance, as there is
no convenient place to pack it, and very likely
much difficulty in cooking it.

1.15.—Marched from eight till one over very
hilly country, mostly burnt.   It seems there are
Boers about ; their laager was seen last night, and
I believe our scouts are now in touch with them.
The pet of the left section, a black and white
terrier named Tiny, has been having a fine hunt
after˙ a hare, to the amusement of the whole
brigade·   She is a game little beast, and follows
us everywhere.   Jacko, of the right section, rides
on a gun-limber.   We passed a farm just now
which was being looted.   Three horsemen have
just passed with a chair each, also picture-frames
(all for fuel, of course), and one man carrying
a huge feather mattress, also fowls and flour.
Artillery don't get much chance at this sort of
game.

(2 P.M.).—Firing began on the right, and
we were trotted up a long steep hill into
action, bullets dropping round, but no one hit.
In front are two remarkable kopjes, squat, steep,

and flat - topped. We are shelling one of them.*

(4.30 P.M.).—This is the warmest work we have had yet. Our waggon is with the guns, unhooked, and we and the team are with the limbers in rear. There is no shelter, for the ground is level. Boer guns on a kopje have got our range, and at one time seemed much interested in our team, for four shells fell in a circle round us, from thirty to forty yards off. It was very unpleasant to sit waiting for the bull's-eye.

(4.35 P.M.).—We have shifted the teams a bit, and got out of the music. To go back : we have been in action all the afternoon, shelling a kopje where the Boers have several guns. It is a wooded one, and they are very difficult to locate. They have a great advantage, as we are on the open level ground below, and they have been fairly raining shells round us. Fortunately most of them burst only on impact, and are harmless,

---

* We were (as we heard long after) in action against De Wet's rear-guard. He had escaped from the cordon just before it was drawn tight, with a small and mobile force, and was now in retreat towards Lindley. Broadwood's cavalry pursued him, but in vain.

owing to the soft ground, outside a very small radius ; they seem to be chiefly segment shell, but I saw a good many shrapnel, bursting high and erratically. The aim was excellent, and well-timed shrapnel would have been very damaging. Still, we have been very lucky even so, only one man wounded, and no guns, waggons or horses touched. Once, when trotting out of action, a shell burst just beside our team—an excellent running shot for the sportsman who fired it ! It made a deafening noise, but only resulted in chipping a scratch on my mare's nose with a splinter. She thought she was killed, and made a great fuss, kicking over the traces, etc. ; so that we had to halt to put things straight.

In this case, again, the veldt was alight every-where, but it was only short grass, and we could trot safely through the thin lambent line of flame. I'm afraid we shall be short of ammunition soon. We started yesterday with only one hundred rounds per gun.

Can it be that De Wet has got round here, and that we are up against his main position ?

What is happening elsewhere I don't know.
There are a lot of cavalry, Yeomanry, infantry,
etc., about somewhere, but here we seem alone
with a small infantry escort, and no sound but
the opposing guns. It shows how little a single
Tommy sees or knows of a fight.

At dark we marched away about a mile, and
bivouacked. Williams and I minced our meat in
one of the battery mincing machines, and made
a grand dish of it over the cook's fire. There
was a red glare over half the sky to-night, as
though a Babylon were burning. It was only a
veldt-fire.

July 17.—*Tuesday.*—Reveillé at six. Our
horses are grazing, harnessed. We are waiting
for the Staff. to say if this is a good position.
It appears that De Wet retreated in the night,
and went towards Lindley, which will complete
the circle of the hunt. Our sections are separated
again. The right, under Lieutenant Lowe, has
gone on with the convoy to Senekal, and we and
the 38th Battery (who have now fresh officers),
and most of the brigade, have taken up a position

just under one of the remarkable kopjes I spoke
of, and are told we shall stay here four days.   I
suppose we are part of some endeavour to
surround De Wet, but the whole operations
seem to get more obscure.   He has played this
game for months in this part of the Free State,
and is no nearer capture.   Thinking over it,
one's mental state during a fight is a strange
paradox.   I suppose it arises from the nature of
my work, but, speaking for myself at least, I
feel no animosity to any one.   Infantry, no
doubt, get the lust of battle, but I don't for
my part experience anything like it, though
gunners tell me they do, which is natural.   One
feels one is taking part in a game of skill at a
dignified distance, and any feeling of hostility
is very impersonal and detached, even when
concrete signs of an enemy's ill-will are paying
us noisy visits.   The fact is—and I fancy this
applies to all sorts and conditions of private
soldiers—in our life in the field, fighting plays
a relatively small part.   I doubt if people at
home realize how much in the background are

its dangers and difficulties. The really absorbing
things are questions of material welfare—sordid,
physical, unromantic details, which touch you
at every turn. Shall we camp in time to dry my
blankets? Biscuit ration raised from three to
three and a half! How can I fill my water-
bottle? Rum to-night! Is there time for a
snooze at this halt? Dare I take my boots off
to-night? Is it going to rain? There are
always the thousand little details connected with
the care of horses and harness, and all along the
ever-present problem of the next meal, and how
to make it meet the demands of your hunger.
I don't mean that one is always *worrying* about
such things. They generally have a most
humorous side, and are a source of great amusement; on the other hand, they sometimes seem
overwhelmingly important. Chiefly one realizes
the enormous importance of food to a soldier.
Shortage of sleep, over-marching, severe fighting,
sink into insignificance beside an empty stomach.
Any infantry soldier will tell you this; and it
is on them, who form the bulk of a field force,

that the strain really tells. Mounted men are better able to fend for themselves. (I should say, that an artillery *driver* has in the field the least tiring work of all, physically; at home, probably the heaviest.) It is the foot-soldier who is the measure of all things out here. In the field he is always at the extreme strain, and any defect of organization tells acutely and directly on him. Knowing what it is to be hungry and tired myself, I can't sufficiently admire these Cork and Yorkshire comrades of ours, in their cheerful, steady marching.

By the way, the General was giving orders close to me this morning. He said to our Major, "Your guns are the best — longest range; go up there." So the Lord Mayor is justified; but the special ammunition is a great difficulty. This, however, is only a matter of organization. As to the guns themselves, we have always understood that the pattern was refused by the War Office some years ago; it would be interesting to know on what grounds. They are very simple, and have some features which are obvious improvements on the 15-pr.

There was a serious alarm of fire just now. There is a high wind, and the grass is unusually long. A fire started due to windward, and came rushing and roaring towards us. We drivers took the horses out of reach, and the gunners and infantry attacked it with sacks, etc. But nothing could stop it, though by great efforts they confined its width, so that it only reached one of our waggons and the watercart, which I don't think are damaged. No sooner well past than fellows began cooking on the hot embers.—Stayed here all day, and unharnessed and picketed in the evening.

July 18.—Reveillé at six, and harnessed up; but did nothing all the morning but graze the horses, and at twelve unharness and groom them. I believe we have to take it in turn with the 38th to be in readiness for instant departure. Firing is heard at intervals. We are, I believe, about twenty miles from Senekal, eighteen from Bethlehem, and thirty from Lindley. We call the place

Bultfontein, from a big farm near, where the General has his head-quarters. Water is bad here ; a thick, muddy pool, used also by cattle and horses.

There has been some to-do about the sugar, and we now draw it separately ourselves, two ounces, and find it goes further. There is enough for the morning mealy porridge, which is very nasty without it.

July 19.—Reveillé at six. Harnessed up. Cleaning lines, and grazing all the morning. Grazing is now practically a standing order in all spare time. I believe it is necessary for the horses ; but it acts as an irksome restraint on the men. When not on the move, we have the three stable-hours as in a standing camp, and often " grouse " over them a good deal ; but the horses are certainly in wonderfully good condi-- tion with the care taken of them. The weather is warmer. Frost at night, but no dew ; and a hot sun all the windless, cloudless day.

Visited a pile of loot taken by some 38th men, and got a lump of home-made Boer soap, in

exchange for some English tobacco. It has a
fatty smell, but makes a beautiful white lather.
They had all sorts of household things, and a
wag was wearing a very *piquante* piece of female
head-gear. In the afternoon I got leave away,
and washed in the muddy pool aforesaid. It
seems odd that it can clean one; but it does.
On the way back found a nigger killing a sheep,
and bought some fat, which is indispensable in
our cooking; if there is any over, we boil it and
use it as butter. We cooked excellent mealy
cakes in it in the evening. "We don't know
where we are" to-day; we had mutton, rice, and
cheese for dinner!

July 20.—Harnessed up as usual at dawn, and
"stood by" all the morning. The rumour now
is that De Wet never went to Lindley at all, but
only a small commando, and that he is at Ficks-
burg, fifty miles away on the Basuto border.
What an eel of a man!

' Clements's brigade arrived to-day from somewhere, and is just visible, camped a few miles
away. The biscuit ration was raised from three

to four and a half to-day. Five is the full
number. Rations are good now. Cooked mutton
is served out at night, and also a portion of raw
mutton. Drawing rations is an amusing scene.
It is always done in the dark, and the corporal
stands at the pot doling out chunks. It is a
thrilling moment when you investigate by touch
the nature of the greasy, sodden lump put into
your hand; it may be all bone, with frills of
gristle on it, or it may be good meat. Complaints are useless; a ruthless hand sweeps you
away, and the *queue* closes up. Later on, a
sheep's carcass (very thin) is thrown down and
hewed up with a bill-hook. There is great
competition for the legs and shoulders, which
are good and tender. If you come off with only
ribs, you take them sadly to the public mincing
machine, and imagine they were legs when you
eat the result. A rather absurd little modicum
of jam is also served out, but it serves to sweeten
a biscuit. There is rum once a week (in theory).
Duff at midday the last few days. It is difficult to
say anything general about rations, because they

vary from day to day, often with startling suddenness, according to the conditions of the campaign.

I was on picket this night, a duty which is 'far
less irksome when in the field than when in a
standing camp. Vigilance is of course not re-
laxed, but many petty rules and regulations are.
There is no guard-tent, of course, in which you
must stay when not on watch ; as long as it is
known where you can be found at a moment's
notice, you are free in the off hours. . You can
be dressed as you like as long as you carry your
revolver.

By the way, I have lost my C.I.V. slouch hat
long ago. It came of wearing a very unnecessary
helmet, merely because it was served out. That
involved carrying the hat in my kit, and it is
wonderful how one loses things on the march,
in the hurried nocturnal packings and unpack-
ings, when every strap and article of kit must be
to your hand in the dark, or you will be late
with your horses and cause trouble. My great
comfort is a Tam-o'-Shanter, which I wear when-
ever we are not in marching order.

As for the revolver, I got into trouble with
the Sergeant-Major this night for parading for
picket without it.   It was not worth while to
explain that I had no ammunition for it ; to
take your " choking-off," and say nothing, is
always the simplest plan.   I once had one
cartridge given me, but lost this precious pos-
session.   I suppose there was some hitch in the
arrangements, for our revolvers are only
cumbrous ornaments.

There are three pickets and a corporal in
charge ; each of the three takes two hours on
and four off, which works out at about four
hours on watch for each, but less if reveillé is
early.   Personally I don't mind the duty much,
even after a long day's march.   On a fine still
night two hours pass quickly in the lines,
especially if one or two picket ropes break,
and the horses get tied up in knots.   If there
is a lack of incident, you can meditate.   Your
head is strangely clear, and for a brief interval
your horizon widens.   In the sordid day it is
often narrowed to a cow's.

July 21.—The same old game ; harnessed up
and remained ready. There was a sudden alarm
about three, and we jumped into our kit, hooked
in, and moved off, only to return in a few minutes.
The General possibly gave the order to see if we
were ready. He reviewed us before we went
back, and seemed pleased. I heard him admiring
the horses, and saying there was plenty of work
in them. "You've been very lucky after that
shell-fire the other day," he said.

A much-needed convoy turned up from
Bethlehem to-day with ammunition for us.
We took our waggon down in the morning
and filled it. A box of matches per man
was also served out. In the evening came
the joyful news that we were to start to-
morrow, two days' fighting expected. Williams
and I made a roaring fire of an ammunition box
in honour of the occasion, and a grand supper
of mealy-cakes and tea, and smoked and talked
till late. Summing up our experiences, we
agreed that we enjoyed the life thoroughly,
but much preferred marching to sitting still.

M

Both thoroughly fit and well, as nearly all have been since campaigning began. In numbers, I hear, we are twenty-two short of our full complement.

One thing that makes a great difference is that campaigning has become routine. One doesn't worry over little things, as one did in early days, when one dreamt of nose-bags, bridoons, muzzles, etc., and the awful prospect of losing something important or unimportant, and when one harnessed-up in a fever of anxiety, dreading that the order "hook in" would find one still fumbling for a strap in the dark, in oblivion of the hot coffee which would be missed cruelly later. In a score of little ways one learns to simplify things, save time, and increase comfort. Not that one ever gets rid of a strong sense of responsibility. Entire charge, day and night, of two horses and two sets of harness, is no light thing.

July 22.—*Sunday.*—Reveillé at six. Boot and saddle at 7.30; started at 8.30—a lovely day. Marched out about three miles with the brigade, and are now halted. An officer has just explained to the non-coms. what is going to happen. The Boer forces are in the mountains east of us, whence there are only three outlets, that is, passes (or neks, as the Dutch call them), one at each corner of a rough triangle. British columns are watching all these, Hunter, Paget, Clements, and Bruce Hamilton. Ours is called Slabbert's Nek, and to-day's move is a reconnaissance in force towards it, without likelihood of fighting. The delay here has been to allow every column to get into position, so that when an attack is made there may be no escape from the trap. The trap, of course, is a very big one, one corner, I believe, being at the Basuto border. Something like a whole army corps is engaged. It is most novel and unusual to know anything about what one is doing. It makes a marvellous difference to one's interest in everything, and I have often wondered why we are not told more. But I suppose the fact is that very few people know.

We halted while the mounted troops made a

long reconnaissance, and then came back to camp. It clouded up in the evening, and about eight began to rain, and suddenly, with no warning, to blow a hurricane. I rushed to my harness, covered up my kit in it, seized my blankets and bolted for a transport-waggon, dived under it, tripping over the bodies of the Collar-maker sergeant and his allies, breathlessly apologized, and disposed myself as best I could. But the rain drove in, and there seemed always to be mules on my feet; so, when fairly wet through, I crept out and joined a circle at a great fire which similar unfortunates had built, where we cooked two camp-kettles full of mysteriously commandeered tea and porridge, and made very merry till reveillé at 4.30 in the morning.

CHAPTER VIII.

SLABBERT'S NEK AND FOURIESBERG.

July 23.—Harnessed up at 4.30, and marched out in a raw, cold fog, all wet, but very cheerful. While halting at the *rendezvous* to await our escort, there were great stories of the night, especially of a tempestuous scene under a big waggon-sheet crowded with irreconcilable interests. We marched straight towards the mountains, ten or twelve miles, I suppose, till we were pretty close up, and then Clements's two great lyddite five-inch guns came into position and fired at long range. They are called "Weary Willie" and "Tired Tim," and each is dragged by twenty-two splendid oxen. We soon moved on a mile or two farther, crossed one of the worst spruits I remember, climbed a very steep hill, and came into action just on its brow, firing at a distant ridge. All this time the infantry had been advancing on either flank in extended order.

(3.30 P.M.)—We and the 38th and the cow-guns, as they are called, have been raining shell on the Boer positions and on their guns. The situation, as I see it, is this : we are exactly oppo-site the mouth of the nek, stretching back into the mountains like a great grass road, bordered with battlements of precipitous rock, which at this end—the gate we are knocking at—swell out on either side into a great natural bastion of bare rock. On these are the Boer trenches, tier above tier, while their guns are posted on the lower ground between. It looks an impregnable position. The Royal Irish, I hear, are attacking the right hand bastion ; the Munsters, I think, the left, and there is a continuous rattle of rifle-fire from both.

Our teams, waggons, and limbers, have been shell-dodging under the brow of the hill. They have fallen all around us, but never on us. One, which I saw fall, killed five horses straight off, and

wounded the Yeomanry chap who was holding
them. We have shifted position two or three
times ; it is windy, and very cold. A new and
unpleasant experience in the shape of a pom-
pom has come upon the scene. Far off you hear
pom-pom-pom-pom-pom, five times, and directly
afterwards, like an echo, pom-pom-pom-pom-pom
in your neighbourhood, five little shells'bursting
over an area of about eighty yards, for all the
world like a gigantic schoolboy's cracker. The
new captain of the unlucky 38th has been hit in
two places by one.

At the close the day was undecided ; the
infantry had taken some trenches, but were still
face to face with others, and fire was hottest at
sunset. But I believe the pom-pom was
smashed up, and a big gun silenced, if not
smashed. We bivouacked where we were, but
desultory rifle-fire went on long after dark.

July 24.—Reveillé at five. Directly after
breakfast we took our waggon back to the convoy
to fill up with shells from the reserve. All the
artillery, including ours, took position again,

and began hammering away, but not for long, as the Boers had been evacuating the whole position in the night, and the last of their trenches was now occupied. I believe the Royal Irish have lost heavily, the Munsters only a few. We got away, and marched through the nek, up and down steep grassy slopes, and through the site of the Boer laager. I was struck by its remarkable cleanliness; I thought that was not a Boer virtue. We halted close to the emplacement where one of the Boer guns had been yesterday. There was a rush to see some horrible human *débris* found in it. I was contented with the word-pictures of enthusiastic gunners, and didn't go myself. From the brow, a glorious view opened out. The nek, flanked by its frowning crags, opened out into an immense amphitheatre of rich undulating pasture-land, with a white farm here and there, half hidden in trees. Beyond rose tier on tier of hills, ending on the skyline in snow-clad mountain peaks. You could just conjecture that a " happy valley " ran right and left. After the scorched monotony of

the veldt it was a wonderful contrast. We camped just where the nek ends, near an empty farm, which produced a fine supply of turkeys, geese, and chickens. The Captain, who has charge of our commissariat, never misses a chance of supplementing our rations. Williams was sent to forage, and for personal loot got some coffee and a file of Boer newspapers, or rather war-bulletins, published in Bethlehem, and roughly lithographed, chiefly lies, I expect.*
The Boers have retired south, deeper into the trap. Poultry was issued, and the gunners and drivers of our waggon drew by lot the most amazing turkey I have ever seen. It had been found installed in a special little enclosure of

* Here is an extract, since translated, from one of these precious "newspapers," which ought to be one day edited in full. It is a telegram from General Snyman at the Boer laager at Mafeking, dated March 2, 1900, when the famous siege had been going on for five months and a half. After some trivial padding about camp details, it concludes : " The bombardment *by the British* (sic) is diminishing considerably. Our burghers are still full of courage. *Their sole desire is to meet the enemy !* " This is only a mild specimen of the sort of intelligence that was allowed to penetrate to a remote farm like this at Slabbert's Nek, whose owner was now fighting us, probably, to judge from these documents, in utter ignorance of the hopelessness of his cause.

its own, and I fear was being fattened for some domestic gala-day which never dawned. It was prodigiously plump.

July 25. — *Wednesday.* — Reveillé at six. Started at 8.30, at the outset crossing a very awkward drift. It was a sort of full dress crossing, so to speak, when all the officers collect and watch the passage. We dived down a little chasm, charged through a river, and galloped up the side of a wall. One waggon stuck, and we had to lend it our leaders. There was a strong, cold wind, and we kept on our cloaks all day ; a bright sun, though, in which I thought the brigade made a very pretty spectacle in its advance, with long streamers of mounted troops and extended infantry on either flank. About one, our section was ordered to march back some miles and meet the rearguard. On the way we passed Hunter and his staff, and his whole brigade, followed by miles of waggons, which we halted to allow to pass, and then followed. They might have discovered they wanted the rearguard strengthening a little

sooner, for the road was very bad, and our
horses had a hard job. The united brigades
camped at sunset. Rumours rife, and one, that
De Wet has cut the line near Kroonstadt, seems
really true. Very cold.

July 26.—Reveillé at 6.30. We waited for
orders all the morning, with the horses hooked in
ready. While sitting by my team I had my hair
cut by a Munster, and an excruciating shave.
Rumour is that the Boers have been given till
two to surrender. Rumour that they have surrendered. Stated as a fact. Rumour reduced
to story that the town of Fouriesberg (five
miles on) has surrendered. Anyway, some
British prisoners have escaped and come in.
Grazing in harness for the rest of the day.

July 27.—Reveillé at 5.15. Hooked in and
waited for the whole convoy to file by, as we
are to be rearguard. It took several hours, and
must be five or six miles long. It was a heavy,
misty day, and some rain fell. Started at last
and marched up the valley, which narrowed considerably here, under the shadow of beetling

cliffs, for about eight miles, with incessant
momentary halts, as always happens in the
rear of a column.   Suddenly the valley opened
out to another noble circle bounded by mountains on all sides, some wearing a sprinkling of
snow still.   Here we came to the pretty little
town of Fouriesberg, and joined the general
camp, which stretched as far as you could see,
thousands of beasts grazing between the various
lines, and interminable rows of outspanned
waggons.   At night camp fires twinkled far into
the distance, and signals kept flashing from
high peaks all round.   An officer has been
telling us the situation, which is that the trap is
closed, the Boers being surrounded on all sides ;
that they are expected to surrender ; that it will
be a Paardeberg on a bigger scale—the biggest
haul of prisoners in the war.

Some commandeered ham was served out, and
we fried ours over the cook's fire with great
success.   I may say that the service mess-tin is
our one cooking utensil, and the work it stands
is amazing ; it is a flat round tin with a handle

and a lid. It is used indiscriminately for boiling, frying, and baking, besides its normal purpose of holding rations.

July 28.—Reveillé at six. After waiting in uncertainty for some time we were left, with the Staffords from Hunter's column, to guard the town, while the other troops moved off. We camped just outside the town, and there was a rush for loot directly, of course only from unoccupied houses, whose rebel owners are fighting. Unhappily others had been there before us, and the place was skinned. But we got a Kaffir cooking-pot, and a lot of fuel, by chopping up a manger in a stable. My only domestic loot was a baby's hat, which I eventually abandoned, and a table and looking-glass which served for fuel. But we found a nice Scotch family in a house, and bought a cabbage from them. There was a dear old lady and two daughters. Williams dropped two leaves of the cabbage, and got a playful rebuke from her. She said he must not waste them, as they were good and tender. By the way, we bought this

cabbage with our last three-penny bit. We had
sovereigns, but they are useless in this country,
for there is no change. These people told us
that they had been ten months prisoners (at
large) of the Boers. Their men had gone to
Basutoland, like many more. They had been
well treated, and suffered little loss, till the
advent of the conquering British, when forty or
fifty hens were taken by Highlanders at night.

A lovely warm afternoon, and for a wonder
freedom till four, the first spell of it for weeks.
Went to a puddle some way off, near a Kaffir
kraal, and washed. Some women came with
calabashes for water, and I tried to buy the
bead bangles and waist-lace off a baby child,
but failed. Then I invaded the kraal for meal
and chickens, but failed again. I never thought,
when I visited Earl's Court a year ago, that I
should look on the African original so soon.
Round mud hovels, with a tall plaited-straw
portico in front. Most of the men look like
worthless loafers; the women finely-built,
capable creatures.

Heavy firing has been going on all day, mostly with lyddite, on our side, by the sound. You can see the shells bursting on the top of a big kopje.

This is a funny little place : pleasant cottages dotted round in desultory fashion, as though the town had been brought up in waggons and just tipped out anyhow. Half the houses are empty and gutted; we are all going to sleep in houses to-night. There has been a row about looting a chemist's shop; our fellows thought he was away with the Boers, but he turned up in the middle. There were some curious bits of plunder.

We are much disappointed at being left out of the fighting to-day, but it's only natural. We are only half a battery, and have no reserve ammunition, actual or prospective, for some time.

I have struck my last match. I have now to rely on cordite, which, however, only acts as a spill. You get a rifle cartridge (there are plenty to be got, the infantry seem to drop them about by hundreds), wrench out the bullet and wad, and find the cordite in long slender threads like vermicelli. You dip this in another man's lighted pipe, when it flares up, and you can light your own.

In the evening Williams and I made a fire, and cooked our cabbage in our Kaffir pot, a round iron one on three legs, putting in meat and some (looted) vinegar. How good it was! It was the first fresh green food we had eaten since leaving England, and it is what one misses most. Two escaped prisoners of the Canadian Mounted Infantry came to our fire, and we had a most interesting chat with them till very late. They spoke highly of the way they had been treated. In food they always fared just as the Boers did, and were under no needlessly irksome restrictions. They said that in this sort of warfare the Boers could always give us points. They laugh at our feeble scouting a mile or two ahead, while their own men are ranging round in twos and threes, often fifteen miles from their commando, and at night venturing right up to our camps. In speed of movement, too, they can beat us; in spite of their heavy bullock transport they can travel at least a third quicker than we. Their discipline was good enough for its purpose. A man would obey a direct order whatever it was. They only wanted a stiffening of our own class of military discipline to make them invulnerable. They sang hymns every night in groups round their fires, " but are hypocrites." (On this point, however, my informants differed a little.) They said the leader of this force was Prinsloo, and that we had not been fighting De Wet at all. It seems there are two De Wets, Piet and Christian. There was a rumour yesterday that Piet had been captured near Kroonstadt, though Christian seems to be the important one. But the whole thing is distracting, like constructing history out of myths and legends.

July 29.—*Sunday.*—Church parade at eleven. It is reported, and is probably true, that the whole Boer force has surrendered. If so we have missed little or nothing. About twenty

N

prisoners came in in the morning, quaint, rough people, shambling along on diminutive ponies. In the afternoon Williams went foraging for the officers, and I visited our Scotch friends, the donors of the cabbage, who were very kind, and asked me in. The married son had just come in from Basutoland, where he had been hiding, a great red, strapping giant, with his wife and babies by him. He had originally been given a passport to allow him to remain neutral, but later they had tried to make him fight, so he ran away, and had been with a missionary over the border, whose house he repaired. It was pleasant to see this joyful home-coming.

Rations to-day, one biscuit and a pound of flour. How to cook it ? Some went to houses, some made dough-nuts (with deadly properties, I believe). No fat and no baking-powder. Fortunately, Williams brought back from his expedition, besides fowls, etc., for the officers, some bread and, king of luxuries, a big pot of marmalade, which he bought from a pretty little Boer girl, the temporary mistress of a fine farm.

Her father, she proudly explained, was away fighting us, " as was his duty." Williams was quite sentimental over this episode. The Canadians came round to our fire again, and we had another long talk. They said there were very few Transvaalers in this army. The Free Staters hate them. The remains we found in the gun-emplacement at Slabbert's Nek were those of Lieutenant Muller, a German artillerist. The Boers always had plenty of our harness, stores, ammunition, etc.

July 30.—After stables Williams and I went foraging in the town and secured scones, a fowl (for a shilling), another cabbage, and best of all, some change, a commodity for which one has to scheme and plot.   We managed it by first getting into a store and buying towels, spoons, notebooks, etc., up to ten shillings, and then cajoling and bluffing a ten-shilling bit out of the unwilling store-keeper. This was changed by the lady who sold us the fowl, an Englishwoman. On our return there was harness-cleaning, interrupted by a sudden order to move, but only to

shift camp about a mile. This is always annoying, because at halts you always collect things
such as fuel and meal and pots, which are impossible to carry with you. Of course this is no
matter, if regular marching and fighting are on
hand, but just for shifting camp it is a nuisance.
However, much may be done by determination.
I induced the Collar-maker to take our flour on
his waggon ; marmalade, meal, etc., were hastily
decanted into small tins, and stuffed into wallets,
and just before starting Williams furtively tossed
the fuel-sack into a buck-waggon, and hitched
up the Kaffir pot somewhere underneath. I
strung a jug on my saddle, which, what with
feed-bags (contents by no means confined to
oats), and muzzles, with meat and things in
them, is rather Christmas-tree-like. We marched
through the town, and to the base of a kopje
about a mile away, where preparations for a big
camp had been made. It is confirmed that the
Boers have surrendered *en masse*, and they are
to be brought here.

After we had unharnessed, I got leave to go

back to town and send a joint telegram home
from a dozen of us. The battery has a tele-
graphic address at home from which wires are
forwarded to our relations. The charge for
soldiers is only 2s. a word, so a dozen of us can
say "quite well" to our relations for about
2s. 8d. The official at the office said the wire
was now open, but that he had no change.
However, he produced 5s. when I gave him £2.
It was a little short, but the change was valuable. He said that to pass the censor it must
be signed by an officer, so I had to look for one.
After some dusty tramping, I found a captain of
the Staffords, saluted, and made my request.
We were, I suppose, about equal in social
station, but I suddenly—I don't know why—felt
what a gulf the service put between us. He was
sleek and clean, and talking about the hour of
his dinner to another one, just as if he were at a
club. I was dirty, unshaven, out at knees, and
was carrying half a sack of fuel—a mission like
this has to serve subsidiary purposes—and felt
like an abject rag-and-bone-picking ruffian. He

took the paper, signed it, and went on about his confounded dinner. However, I expect mine rivalled his for once in a way, for when I got back one of the "boys" (nigger drivers) had cooked our chicken and cabbage, and we ate it, followed by scones and marmalade, and, to wind up with, black coffee, made from some rye coffee given us by one of our Canadian prisoner friends. I had met one of them near the telegraph office, and visited his quarters. Rye makes remarkably good strong coffee, with a pleasant burnt taste in it. The camp had filled up a bit, the Manchesters, Staffords and 2nd Field Battery, of Rundle's division, having come in. We also played with flour and fat over our fire, and made some chupatties. The Captain had sent a foraging party out to secure fat at any price. Quite a warm night. A deep furrow passed near my harness, and I had a most comfortable bed in it.

July 31.—The first batch of 250 prisoners have come in, and are herded near. They are of all ages from sixty to fifteen, dressed in all varieties of rough plain clothes, with some ominous exceptions in the shape of a khaki tunic, a service overcoat, etc. Some seemed depressed, some jocular, the boys quite careless. All were lusty and well fed. Close by were their ponies, tiny little rats of things, dead-tired and very thin. Their saddles were mostly very old, with canvas or leather saddle-bags, containing cups, etc. I saw also one or two horses with our regimental brands on them. Some had bright-coloured rugs on them, and all the men had the same, which lent vivid colour to the otherwise sombre throng.

We watered and grazed near an outlying picket, and saw many prisoners coming in in twos and threes, and giving up their rifles. What will they do with them ? They are nominally rebels since the 15th of June ; but I doubt if a tenth of them ever heard of Roberts's proclamation. Communications are few in this big, wild country ; and their leaders systematically deceive them. Besides, to call the country conquered when Bloemfontein was taken, is absurd. The real fighting had not begun then,

and whole districts such as this were unaffected.
It seems to me that morally, if not legally, these
people are fair-and-square civilized belligerents,
who have fought honestly for their homes, and
treated our prisoners humanely. Deportation
over-sea and confiscation of farms seem hard
measures, and I hope more lenience will be
shown.

In the evening Doctor Moon, of the Hamp-
shire Yeomanry, a great friend of Williams,
turned up, and had supper with us. We had
no fatted calf to kill; but fortunately could
show a tolerable *menu*, including beef and
marmalade.

I was on picket this night. About midnight
a lot of Boer prisoners, and a long train of their
ox-waggons, began coming in. It was very
dark, and they blundered along, knocking down
telegraph posts, and invading regimental lines,
amidst a frightful din from the black drivers,
and a profane antiphony between two officers,
of the camp and the convoy respectively.

In my second watch, in the small hours, a

Tommy with a water-cart strayed into our lines,
asking for the Boer prisoners, for whom he had
been sent to get water. He swore copiously at
the nature of his job in particular, and at war in
general. I showed him the way, and consoled
him with tobacco.

August 1.—Grazing and harness-cleaning all
day. More prisoners came in, and also our old
friends the Munsters, and General Paget.
Rumours galore. We are going to Cape Town
with the prisoners; to Harrismith; to Winberg;
to the Transvaal on another campaign, etc.
Definite orders came to move the next morning. In the evening an unusual flood of odds
and ends of rations was poured on us; flour, a
little biscuit, a little fat for cooking, diminutive
hot potatoes, a taste of goose, commandeered the
same day by the mounted gunners, a little
butter from the same source, besides the usual
sugar, cooked meat, and tea. Drawing from
this *cornucopia* was a hard evening's work. We
also got hold of some dried fruit-chips, and as a
desperate experiment tried to make a fruit

pudding, wrapping the fruit in a jacket of dough and baking it in fat in our pot. The result, seen in the dark, was a formless black mass, very doughy and fatty; but with oases of palatable matter.

CHAPTER IX.

TO PRETORIA.

August 2.—Reveillé at six. Harnessed up, and started out to join the brigade and its long column of prisoners, mounted on their ponies, and each leading another with a pack on it. We only went about seven miles (back towards the Nek), and camped at midday. I had been suffering from toothache for some days, and was goaded into asking the doctor to remove the offender. He borrowed a forceps from the R.A.M.C. and had it out in a minute. The most simple and satisfactory visit to the dentist I have ever had. No gloomy fingering of the illustrated papers, while you wait your turn with the other doomed wretches, no horrible accessories of padded chair and ominous professional plant ; just the open sunny veldt, and a waggon pole to sit on! In the evening I got some 38th fellows to cook us some chupatties of our flour. They treated me to fried liver over their fire, and we had a jolly talk. It is said that we are to take the prisoners to Winberg, and then go to the Transvaal. Cold night; hard frost.

August 3.—Reveillé at six. Sunrise this day was peculiarly beautiful; a milky-blue haze lay in festoons along the hills, and through this the sun shot a delicate flush on the rocks and grassy slopes, till the farther side of the valley looked unreal as a dream.

Started at nine; marched as far as the inward end of the Nek, and camped. I got a splendid wash, almost a bath, in a large pond, in the company of many Boer prisoners, who, I am bound to say, seemed as anxious for cleanliness as we were. I talked to two most charming young men, who discussed the war with me with perfect freedom and urbanity. They dated their *débâcle* from Roberts's arrival, and the use of flanking movements with large

numbers of mounted men. They made very
light of lyddite, and laughed at the legend that
the fumes are dangerous. In action they leave
all their horses in the rear, unwatched, or with
a man or two. (Our mounted infantry leave a
man to every four horses.) I asked if a small
boy, who was sitting near, fought. They said,
" Yes: a very small stone suffices to shelter
him." They talked very good English.

The right section have turned up and, I hear,
are camped about two miles away. They have
been a fortnight away doing convoy work, to
Senekal, Winberg, and back. They brought us
no mails, to our great disappointment. We
have had no letters now since June 15th.
Strange rumours come in about 40,000 troops
going to China. A very cold night; I should
say 15 degrees of frost.

August 4.—Did a rapid five hours' march
through the Nek, and back to Bultfontein,
as part of the advance-guard. On the way we
picked up the right section, and exchanged our
experiences. They had had no fighting, but a

very good time. They had distractingly luscious
stories of duff, rum, and jam at Winberg, and
all looked very fat and well. We camped,
unharnessed, and watered at the same old
muddy pool, muddier than ever. I visited an
interesting trio of guns which were near us, in
charge of Brabant's Horse; one was German,
one French, one British. The German was a
Boer gun captured the other day, a 9-pr. Krupp,
whose bark we have often heard. It has a very
long range, 8000 yards, but otherwise seemed
clumsy compared with ours, with a cumbersome
breech action and elevating gear. The French one
was a Hotchkiss, made by the French company,
belonging to Brabant's Horse—a smart little
weapon, but not so handy, I should say, as ours.
The British one was a 15-pr. field gun, of the 77th
Field Battery, lost at Stormberg and recaptured
the other day. It had evidently had hard and
incessant use, and was much worn. Brabant's
Horse were our escort to-day, a fine, seasoned
body of rough, wild-looking fellows, wearing a
very noticeable red puggaree round their slouch

hats. They are fine scouts, and accomplished marauders, for which the Boers hate them. Jam for tea, and milk in the tea—long unknown luxuries, which the right section brought with them. In the evening I went to a sing-song the 38th gave round their camp fire. It was very pleasant, and they were most hospitable to us.

August 5.—Reveillé at five. Harnessed up; but some hitch ahead occurred, and we unhooked, watered, and grazed. Finally started about 8.30, and made a rapid march as advance guard, of about fourteen miles, with only momentary halts. Country very hilly; steep, squat, flat-topped kopjes and several bad drifts. We camped about 1.30 near five small houses in a row, with the novel accessory of some big trees— probably a town in large letters on the map. It appears the convoy has halted some way back for the four midday hours dear to the oxen. The rest of the column came in at dusk. A warm night. Every night in camp you may hear deep-throated choruses swelling up from

the prisoners' laager. The first time I heard
it I was puzzled to know what they were singing ; the tune was strangely familiar, but I could
not fix it. It was not till the third night that
I recognized the tune of "O God, our help,"
but chanted so slowly as to be difficult to
catch, with long, luxurious rests on the high
notes, and mighty, booming crescendos. Coming
from hundreds of voices, the effect was sometimes very fine. At other times smaller groups
sang independently, and the result was a
hideous noise. I wonder if the words corre-
spond to our tune. If so, every night these
prisoners, who have staked and lost all in a
hopeless struggle, sing, "O God, our help in
ages past." This is faith indeed.

August 6.—Bank Holiday.—At 6.45 we
started as advance-guard again, and marched
for five and a half hours, with only a halt or
two of a few minutes, to Senekal. The country
gradually became flatter, the kopjes fewer and
lower, till at last it was a great stretch of arid,
dusty plain. It seemed quite strange to be

driving on level ground, after endless hills and
precipitous drifts. We and Brabant's Horse were
advance guard, and clattered down in a pall
of blinding white dust into a substantial little
tin-roofed town, many stores open, and people
walking about in peace (the ladies all in black).
Full of soldiers, of course, but still it was our
first hint for months of peace and civilization,
and seemed home-like. One of the first things I
saw was a jar of Osborne biscuits in a window,
and it gave me a strange thrill! The convoy
and prisoners follow this evening. The column
is miles long, as besides our own transport,
there are all the Boer waggons, long red ones,
each with some prisoners on it and a soldier.
Also scores of Cape carts, with a fat farmer in
each. There was a wild rush for provisions in
the town by our orderlies and Brabant's. They
got bread, and I bought some eggs and jam on
commission. After camping and unharnessing,
I had a good wash in the river, an orange-
coloured puddle. I wonder how it is that by some
fatality there is always a dead quadruped, mule,

o

horse, or bullock, near our washing places. We
don't mind them on the march; they are dotted
along every road in South Africa now, I should
think; but when making a refreshing toilette they
jar painfully. Kipling somewhere describes a
subtle and complex odour, which, he says, is the
smell of the great Indian Empire. That of the
great African Empire in this year of grace is the
direct and simple one which I have indicated.
In the evening we had a grand supper of fried
eggs, jam, chupatties, and cocoa. This meal
immediately followed tea. We made our fire
in the best place for one, an ant-hill, about two
feet high. The plan is to hack two holes, one
in the top, another on the windward side, and
to connect the two passages. There is then a fine
draught, and you can cook both on the top and
at the side. Inside, the substance of the hill
itself gets red-hot and keeps a sustained heat.

Recipe for jam chupatties.—Take some suet
and melt rapidly in a mess-tin, over a quick fire
(because you are hungry and can't wait); meanwhile make a tough dry dough of flour and water

and salt ; cut into rounds to fit the mess-tin
spread with jam, double over and place in the
boiling fat ; turn them frequently. Cook for
about ten minutes. A residual product of this
dish is a sort of hard-bake toffee, formed by the
leakage of jam from the chupatties.

Brabant's Horse left in the night.

August 7.—A bitterly cold, windy day.
Marched for several hours over a yellow, undulating plain and camped, near nothing, about
12.30. After dinner I walked over to a Kaffir
kraal and bought fuel, and two infants'
copper bangles. I was done over the bangles,
so I made it up over the fuel (hard round
cakes of prepared cow's dung), filling a sack
brim-full, in spite of the loud expostulations
of the black lady. They were a most amusing
crowd, and the children quite pretty. I also
tasted Kaffir beer for the first, and last, time.
Kaffir bangles abound in the Battery. In fact,
you will scarcely see a soldier anywhere without
them. The fashion is to wear them on the wrist
as bracelets. They are of copper and brass, and

often of beautiful workmanship. The difficulty about collecting curios is that there is nowhere to carry them, though some fellows have a genius for finding room for several heavy bits of shell, etc. Empty pom-pom shells, which are small and portable, are much sought after; and our own brass cartridge, if one could take an old one along, would make a beautiful lamp-stand at home. Rum to-night.

August 8.—Reveillé at six. Off at 7.30. Another march over the same bare, undulating plain. About eleven we passed a spruit where there was a camp of infantry and the 9th Field Battery, who told us they came out when we did, but had only fired four rounds since ! Near here there was a pathetic incident. A number of Boer women met us on the road, all wearing big white linen hoods; they stood in sad groups, or walked up and down, scanning the faces of the prisoners (we were with the main body to-day) for husbands, brothers, sweethearts. Many must have looked in vain. The Boers have systematically concealed losses even from the relatives themselves; and one of the saddest things in this war must be the long torture of uncertainty suffered by the womenfolk at home.

We camped at twelve near a big dam, and unharnessed, but only for a rest, resuming the march at about three, and halting for the night about ten miles farther on. A profligate issue of rations—five biscuits, four ounces of sugar (instead of two or three), duff and rum again. A lovely, frosty night, the moon full, delicate mists wreathing the veldt, hundreds of twinkling camp-fires, and the sound of psalms from the prisoners' laager.

August 9.—In to-day's march the character of the country changed, with long, low, flat-topped kopjes on either side of us, and the road in a sharp-cut hollow between them, covered with loose round stones—a parched and desolate scene. After about ten miles we descended through a long ravine into Winberg, with its red-brick, tin-roofed houses baking in the sun. We skirted the town, passing through long lines of soldiers come to see the prisoners arrive, and out about a mile on to a dusty, dreary plain, where we camped. We were all thrilling with hopes of letters. (Winberg is at the end of a branch of railway, and we are now in touch with the world again.) Soon bags of letters arrived, but not nearly all we expected. I only got those of one mail, but they numbered thirteen, besides three numbers of the *Weekly Times*, and a delightful parcel from home. I sat by my harness in the sun, and read letters luxuriously. It was strange to get news again, and strike suddenly into this extraordinary Chinese *imbroglio*. It appears the war is still going on in the Transvaal, and the rumour is that we shall be sent there straight. Among other news it seems that the H.A.C. are sending the Battery a draft of twenty men from home, to bring us up to strength. I heard from my brother at Standerton, dated July 21. He was with Buller; had not done much fighting yet; was fit and well. There was a disturbance just at dusk, caused by a big drove of Boer ponies, which were being driven into town, getting out of hand

and running amok in the lines of the 38th. Wrote a letter home by moonlight. Very cold, after a hot day. I should think the temperature often varies fifty degrees in the twenty-four hours. Some clothing served out; I got breeches and boots. I wish I could get into the town. There are several things I badly want, though, as usual, the home parcel supplied some.

August 10.—We were rather surprised to hear we might move that day, and must hold ourselves in readiness. We all much wanted to buy things, but there was no help for it. Had a field-day at button-sewing and letter-writing. At eleven there was harness-cleaning, and I was sadly regarding a small remnant of dubbin and my dusty girths and leathers, when the order came for " boot and saddle," and that little job was off. In the end we did not start till three, and marched with the whole brigade nine miles, with one five-minute halt, through easy country, with an unusual number of clumps of trees, and camped just at dusk, near a pool, unharnessed and watered. There was a curious and beautiful sight just before, the sun sinking red into the veldt straight ahead, and the moon rising golden out of it straight behind us. It seems we are bound to Smalldeel, a station on the main line, now eleven miles off. We left all the prisoners at Winberg. Some chaps bought schamboks, saddle-bags, and spurs from them, but being stableman, I hadn't time. I write this by moonlight, crouching close to a fine wood fire, 10 P.M. Well, I shall turn in now.

August 11.—Reveillé at 5.45. We started at eight, and marched the remaining eleven miles in a blinding dust-storm, blown by a gale of cutting wind right in our faces. My eyes were sometimes so bunged up that I couldn't see at all, and thanked my stars I was not driving leads. The worst march we have had yet. About 11.30 we came to the railway, and groped through a dreary little tin village round a station, built on dust, and surrounded by bare, dusty veldt. This was Smalldeel. There was a general rush to the stores after dinner, as we hear we are to entrain for Pretoria to-morrow.

To-day we revolutionized our harness by giving up our off-saddles, our kit to be carried on a waggon. Some time before centre and lead horses had been relieved of breeching and breast-strap, which of course are only needed for wheelers. In the ordinary way all artillery horses are so harnessed that they can be used as wheelers at any moment. The off horse is now very light therefore, having only collar, traces, and crupper, with an improvised strap across the back to support the traces. Of course there are always "spare wheelers," ready-harnessed, following each subdivision in case of casualties. As far back as Bethlehem we discarded big bits also and side-reins, which are quite useless, and waste time in taking in and out when you want to water rapidly, or graze for a few moments. The harness is much simplified now, and takes half the time to put on. The mystery is why it is ever considered necessary to have so much on active service, or even at home, unless to keep drivers from getting too much leisure. Several houses

in this place have been wrecked, and many
fellows slept under the shells. In one of them a
man was selling hot coffee in the evening, at 6*d.*
a cup. It was a striking scene, which I shall
always remember—a large building, floorless
and gutted inside, and full of heaps of rubble,
very dimly lit by a couple of lanterns, in the
light of which cloaked and helmeted figures
moved. I thought of sleeping in a house, for
it was the coldest night I remember; but habit
prevailed, and I turned in as usual by my harness.
The horses have got a head-rope-eating epidemic,
and seemed to be loose all night.

August 12.—*Sunday.*—Reveillé at six. Harnessed up, and waited for orders to entrain for
Pretoria. The 38th Battery have gone already,
and the Wilts Yeomanry. A draft of twenty new
men from England came in by train. They
looked strangely pale and clean and tidy beside
our patched and soiled and sunburnt selves.
Marched down to station, and were entraining
guns, waggons, horses, etc., till about four. The
usual exciting scenes with mules, but it all seems

routine now. Our subdivision of thirty men
were packed like herrings into an open truck,
also occupied by a gun and limber.

August 13.—I write sitting wedged among my
comrades on the floor of the truck, warm sun
bathing us after an Arctic night, and up to my
knees in kit, letters, newspapers, parcels, boxes
of cigarettes, chocolate, etc., for all our over-due
mails have been caught up in a lump somewhere,
and the result of months of affection and thought-
ful care in distant England are heaped on us all
at once. I have about thirty letters. It is an
orgie, and I feel drunk with pleasure. All the
time the train rolls through the wilderness,
with its myriad ant-hills, its ribbon of empty
biscuit tins and dead horses, its broken bridges,
its tiny outpost camps, like frail islands in the
ocean, its lonely stations of three tin houses,
and nothing else beyond, no trees, fields, houses,
cattle, signs of human life. We stopped all
last night at Zand River. All trains stop at
night now, for the ubiquitous De Wet is a
terror on the line. To-day we passed the

charred and twisted remains of another train
he had burnt; graves, in a row, close to it.
Williams and I slept on the ground outside
the truck, after feeding and watering horses
and having tea. It was an uneasy slumber, on
dust and rubble, interrupted once by the train
quietly steaming away from beside us. But it
came back. We were off again at 4.30 A.M., a
merry crowd heaped together under blankets on
the floor of the truck. We ground slowly on
all day, and halted for the night at Viljoen's
Drift, the frontier station.

August 14.—Sleepy heads rose from a sea
of blankets, and blinked out to see the crossing
of the Vaal river, and a thin, sleepy cheer hailed
this event; then we relapsed and waited for the
sun. When it came, and we thawed and looked
about, we saw an entire change of country; hills
on both sides, trees here and there, and many
farms. Soon the upper works of a mine showed,
and then more, and all at once we were in a
great industrial district. At Elandsfontein, the
junction for Johannesburg, we had a long halt,

and a good breakfast, getting free coffee from a huge boiling vat.

(9 P.M.)—We reached Pretoria just at dusk, the last five miles or so being a very pretty run through a beautiful pass, with woods and real *green* fields in the valley, a refreshing contrast to the outside veldt. We detrained by electric light, and bivouacked in an open place just outside the station. I write this in the station bar, where some of us have been having a cup of tea. Paget's Brigade are all here, and I hear Roberts is to review us to-morrow. A Dublin Fusilier, who had been a prisoner since the armoured-train affair at Estcourt until Roberts reached Pretoria, told us we "had a good name here," for Bethlehem, etc. He vaguely talked of Botha and Delarey "dodging round" near here. We have heard nothing of the outside world for a long time, and as far as I can make out, the Transvaal has still to be conquered, just as the Free State has had to be, long after the capture of both capitals.

August 15.—I had gone to sleep in splendid

isolation under the verandah of an empty house, but awoke among some Munsters, who greeted dawn with ribald songs. Harnessed up after breakfast, and marched off through the town, past the head-quarters, where Roberts reviewed us and the 38th. He was standing with a large Staff at the foot of the steps. The order "eyes right" gave us a good view of him, and very small, fit, and alert he looked.

> " 'E's little, but 'e's wise,
> 'E's a terror for 'is size."

I liked what we saw of the town, broad boulevards edged with trees, and houses set back deep in gardens; the men all in khaki uniforms, or niggers, but a good many English ladies and nurses. We marched to a camp on the top of a hill outside the town, and joined the rest of the brigade. A lovely view of the town from here, in a hollow of encircling hills, half-buried in trees, looking something like Florence in the distance. I can hardly believe we are really here when I think of the hopeless depression of June and May at Bloemfontein. Much to our disgust, we weren't allowed to go down to the town in the afternoon. However, we visited a reservoir instead, where a pipe took away the overflow, and here we got a real cold bath in limpid water, on a shingly bottom, a delicious experience. After evening stables Williams and I got leave to go down to town. We passed through broad tree-bordered streets, the central ones having fine shops and buildings, but all looking dark and dead, and came to the Central Square, where we made for the Grand Hotel, and soon found ourselves dining like gentlemen at tables with table-cloths and glasses and forks, and clean plates for every course. The complexity of civilized paraphernalia after the simplicity of a pocket-knife and mess-tin, was quite bewildering. The room was full of men in khaki. Heavens! how hungry that dinner made me! We ordered a bottle of claret, the cheapest being seven shillings. The waiter when he brought it up paused mysteriously, and then, in a discreet whisper to Williams, said he supposed we were sergeant-majors, as none under that rank could be served with wine. Gunner Williams smilingly reassured him, and Driver Childers did his best to look like a sergeant-major, with, I fear, indifferent success. Anyway the waiter was easily satisfied, and left us the claret, which, as there were three officers at the table, was creditable to him. We walked home about 8.30, the streets all silent as death, till we were challenged by a sentry near the outskirts of the town, and asked for the countersign, which we didn't know. There were muttered objections, into which a bottle of whisky mysteriously entered, and we bluffed it out. I have never found ignorance of a countersign a serious obstacle.

August 16.—Grazing most of the morning, during which I have managed to get some letters written, but I have great arrears to make up. Several orders countermanding one another have been coming in, to the general effect that we are probably to start somewhere to-day. The usual crop of diverse rumours as to our future. One says we go to Middelberg, another Lydenberg, another Petersberg. There seem to be several

forces of Boers still about, and De Wet, who
ought to become historic as a guerilla warrior, is
still at large, nobody knows where. I only
trust our ammunition-supply will be better
managed this time. Anyway, we are all fit and
well, and ready for anything, and the horses
in first-class order. I forgot to say that I had
to part with one of my pair, the riding-horse, a
few days before we reached Smalldeel. He was
taken for a wheeler in our team. I now ride the
mare and lead my new horse, which is my old
friend the Argentine, whose acquaintance I first
made at Capetown. Hard work has knocked
most of the vice out of her, though she still is a
terror to the other horses in the lines. She
looks ridiculously small in artillery harness, but
works her hardest, and is very fit, though she
declines to oats unless I mix them with mealies,
which I can't always do.

CHAPTER X.

WARMBAD.[*]

August 16, *continued.*—We started at 4 P.M., and had a most tedious march for about four miles only, with incessant checks, owing to the badness of the ground, so that we arrived long after dark at the camping-ground in indifferent humour. We had followed a narrow valley in a northerly direction. Most of the transport waggons, including our own, stuck in a drift some way back, so that we had no tea, and the drivers no blankets to sleep in (gunners carry their kit on the gun-carriages

[*] In this new campaign Paget's Brigade was, in conjunction with the forces of Baden-Powell, Plumer, and Hickman, to scour the district whose backbone is the railway line running due north from Pretoria to Petersberg. He was to occupy strategic points, isolate and round up stray commandos, and generally to engage the attention of the enemy here, while the grand advance under Roberts and Buller was taking place eastward.

and limbers and ammunition-waggons). However, I got up at midnight and found the kit-
waggon had arrived, and got mine ; also some
tea from a friendly cook of the 38th, so I did
well.

August 17.—Reveillé at 4.15. Started at
five, and to our surprise marched back about a
mile and a half. Picked up the rest of our
buck-waggons on the way, and halted for a
hurried breakfast at dawn. Then marched
through what I hear is called Wonderboom
Port, a narrow nek between two hills, leading
due north, to judge by the sun. We forded a
girth-deep river on the way. The nek led out
on to a long, broad valley, about six miles in
width, bordered on the Pretoria side with a
line of steep kopjes, and on the north by low
brown hills. Long yellow grass, low scrub,
and thorny trees, about the size of hawthorns ;
no road, and the ground very heavy.

(2 P.M.)—We are halted to feed. There is
some firing on the left front. Had a good sleep
for an hour. Later on we went into action, but

never fired, and in the evening marched away behind a hill and camped. The Wilts and Montgomery Yeomanry are with us, and at the common watering-place, a villainous little pool, with a steep, slippery descent to it, I recognized Alexander Lafone, of the latter corps. I walked to their lines after tea, found him sergeant of the guard, and we talked over a fire. We had last seen one another as actors in some amateur theatricals in a country town at home. They had been in action for the first time that day, and had reported 500 Boers close by. A warm night. Quite a change of season has set in.

August 18.—A big gun was booming not far off, during breakfast. A hot, cloudless day. Started about 8.30, and marched till twelve, crossing the valley diagonally, till we reached some kopjes on the other side. A pom-pom of ours is now popping away just ahead, and there is a good deal of rifle-fire.

'(3.15.)—The old music has begun, a shell coming screeching overhead and bursting behind us. We and the convoy were at once moved to a position close under a kopje between us and the enemy. Shells are coming over pretty fast, but I don't see how they can reach us here. A most curious one has just come sailing very slowly overhead, and growling and hiccoughing in the strangest way. I believe it was a ricochet, having first hit the top of the kopje. When it fell there was a rush of gunners to pick up the fragments. I secured one, and it turned out to be part of a huge forty-pounder siege-gun shell. Such a gun would far out-range ours, and I believe the scouts have not located it yet, which explains our inactivity.

(3.30.)—Our right section has gone into action, and is firing now. Some wounded Yeomen just brought in. One of them, I'm sorry to say, is Lafone, with a glancing wound under the eye, sight uninjured. We camped at five, and unharnessed. It seems the Yeomanry lost ten men prisoners, but the Boers released them after taking their rifles.

August 19.—*Sunday.*—Reveillé at four. Some days are very irritating to the soldier, and this

was a typical one. We harnessed up and stood
about waiting for orders for five hours. At last
we moved off, only to return again immediately;
again moved off, and after a few minutes halted ;
finally got more or less started, and marched
five or six miles, with incessant short halts, at
each of which the order is to unbuckle wither-
straps and let horses graze. This sounds simple,
but is a horrible nuisance, as the team soon gets
all over the place, feet over traces, collars over
ears, and so on, if not continually watched and
pulled about. When it is very hot and you are
tired, it is very trying to the temper. At one
halt you think you will lunch. You get out a
Maconochie, open it, and take a spoonful, when
you find the centres tying themselves up in a
knot with the leaders. Up you get, straighten
them out, and sit down again. After two more
spoonfuls, you find the wheelers playing cat's-
cradle with the centres' traces. Perhaps the
wheel-driver is asleep, and you get up and put
them right. Then the grazing operations of the
leaders bring them round in a circle to the

wheelers. Up you get, and finally, as the fifth
spoonful is comforting a very empty stomach,
you hear, "Stand to your horses!" "Mount!"
You hurriedly stuff the tin into a muzzle hanging from the saddle, where you have leisure
to observe its fragrant juices trickling out, stick
the spoon under a wallet-strap, buckle up wither-
straps, and mount. At the next halt you begin
again, and the same thing happens. It is a
positive relief to hear the shriek of a shell, and
have something definite to do or interest you.
About two the 38th fired a few shots at some
Boers on the sky-line, and then we came to
Waterval, where we camped and watered. The
Petersberg railway runs up here, and this was a
station on it, with a few houses besides. Its
only interest is the cage in which several
thousand English prisoners were kept, till
released by Roberts' arrival. I visited it on
the way to a delicious bathe in the river after
tea. It is a large enclosure, full of the remains
of mud huts, and fitted with close rows of tall
iron posts for the electric light, which must have

turned night into day.   It is surrounded by an
elaborate barbed-wire entanglement.   In one
place was a tunnel made by some prisoners to
escape by.   It began at a hole inside a hut, and
ran underground for quite forty yards, to a
point about five yards outside the enclosure.
Some of our chaps passed through it.   In a
large tin shed near the enclosure was a fine
electric-lighting plant for lighting this strange
prison on the open veldt.

This morning the Captain came back, to our
great delight.   He had been away since Winberg, getting stores for us at Bloemfontein.   He
brought a waggon full of clothing and tobacco,
which was distributed after we had come in.
There were thick corduroy uniforms for winter
use.   If they had reached us in the cold weather
they would have been more useful.   It is hot
weather now; but a light drill tunic was also
served out, and a sign of the times was stewed
dry fruit for tea.   The ration now is five
biscuits (the full ration) and a Maconochie, or
bully beef.   Only extreme hunger can make

me stomach Maconochies now. They are quite
sound and good, but one gets to taste nothing
but the chemical preservative, whatever it is.
We have had no fresh meat for a long time
back, but one manages with an occasional change
of bully beef or a commandeered chicken.

The camp is a big one, for infantry reinforcements have come in, and two cow-guns.

August 20.—There was no hour appointed
for reveillé overnight, but we were wakened by
the pickets at 2.30 A.M. At once harnessed up,
and marched off without breakfast. Went north
still, as yesterday, following the railway. Dawn
came slow, silent, and majestic into the cloudless
sky, where a thin sickle of waning moon hung.
It was a typical African dawn, and I watched
every phase of it to-day with care. Its chief
feature is its gentle unobtrusiveness. About
an hour before sunrise, the east grows faintly
luminous ; then just one arc of it gradually and
imperceptibly turns to faint yellow, and then
delicate green ; but just before the sun tops the
veldt there is a curious moment, when all colour

fades out except the steel blue of a twilight sky, and the whole firmament is equally lighted, so that it would be hard to say where the sun was going to rise. The next moment, a sharp rim of dazzling gold cuts the veldt, and in an instant it is broad day. The same applies to sunset. There are no " fine sunsets " here, worthy of Ruskinian rhapsodies ; they are just exquisitely subtle transitions from day to night. But, of course, directly the sun is below the horizon, night follows quickly, as in all countries in these latitudes. There is very little twilight.

(9.30 A.M.)—The country we cross is studded thickly with small trees. . About 6.30 the enemy's rifle-fire began on our front. Our side at first answered with pom-poms, Maxims, and rifle-fire, but our guns have just come into action. The enemy's position appears to be a low ridge ahead covered with bush.—I fancy they were only a skirmishing rear-guard, for after' a bit of shrapnel-practice we moved on, and had a long, tiring day of slow marching and halting, with scattered firing going on in front

and on the flanks. The country must demand
great caution, for the bush is thick now, and whole
commandos might be concealed anywhere. The
Wilts Regiment (some companies of which are
brigaded with us) lost several men and an
officer. We camped on an open space just at
dark. Watering was a long, tiresome business,
from buckets, at a deep, rocky pool. There
were snipers about, and a shot now and then
during the evening.

August 21.—We harnessed up at four; but
waited till seven to move off. This is always
tiresome, as drivers have to stay by their horses
all the time; but of course it is necessary that
in such a camp, with the enemy in the bush near,
all the force should be ready to move at an early
hour. The nights are warm now, but there
is a very chilly time in the small hours. We
marched through the same undulating, wooded
country, crossing a brute of a drift over a river,
where we hooked in an extra pair of horses to
our team. In the summer this must be a lovely
region, when the trees and grass are green; very

like the New Forest, I should think. We had a long halt in the middle of the day, and then marched on till five, when we camped. We waited till eight for tea, as the buck-waggons had stuck somewhere; but I made some cocoa on a fire of mealy-stalks. I forgot to say that Baden-Powell has joined the column with a mounted force and the Elswick Battery, and is now pushing on ahead. I hear that Paget's object is to prevent De Wet from joining Botha, and that Baden-Powell has seized some drift ahead over which he must pass. Fancy De Wet up here! An alternative to Maconochie was issued to-day, in the shape of an excellent brand of pressed beef.

August 22.—Reveillé at 3 A.M. for the right section, who moved off at once, and at 3.45 for my section. We started at 5.30, and marched pretty quickly all the morning to Pynaar's River, which consists of a station on the railway, and a few gutted houses. A fine iron bridge over the river had been blown up, and was lying with its back broken in the water. We camped here about

one, and thought we were in for a decent rest,
after several very short nights. I ate something, and was soon fast asleep by my saddle ;
but at three " harness up " was ordered, and off
we went, but only for a few hundred yards,
when the column halted, and after wasting two
hours in the same place, moved back to camp
again. One would like to know the Staff secrets
now and then in *contretemps* like this ; but no
doubt one cause is the thick bush, which makes
the enemy's movements difficult to follow. Rum
to-night. We went to bed without any orders
for reveillé, which came with vexatious suddenness at 10.45 P.M. I had had about two hours'
sleep. Up we got, harnessed up, hooked in, and
groped in the worst of tempers to where the
column was collecting, wondering what was up
now. We soon started—no moon and very dark
—on a road composed of fine, deep dust, which
raised a kind of fog all round, through which I
could barely see the lead-driver's back. The
order was no talking, no smoking, no lights, and
we moved silently along under the stars, wrapped

in darkness and dust. Happily the road was level, but night marching is always rather trying work for a driver. One's nerves are continually on edge with the constant little checks that occur. The pair in front of you seem to swim as you strain your eyes to watch the traces, and keep the team in even draught; but, do what you can, there is a good deal of jerking into the collar, and narrow shaves of getting legs over traces. Once I saw the General's white horse come glimmering by and melt into the darkness. About 3.30 A.M. lights and fires appeared ahead, and we came on the camp of some other force of ours, all ready to start; soldiers' figures seen silhouetted against the dancing light of camp fires, and teams of oxen in the gloom beyond. A little farther on the column stopped, and we were told we should be there two hours. We fed the horses, and then lit fires of mealy-stalks, and cooked cocoa, and drowsed. At six our transport-waggons came up, and we got our regular breakfast. Then we rode to water, and now (August 23) I am

sitting in the dust by the team, writing this.
There was a stir and general move just now. I
got up and looked where all eyes were looking,
and saw a solitary Boer horseman issuing from the
bush, holding a white flag. An orderly galloped
up to him, and the two went into a hut where
the General is. The rumour is that a thousand
Boers want to surrender.—Rumour reduces
number to one Boer.

In the end we stopped here all day, and what
in the world our forced march was for, is one of
the inexplicable things that so often confront the
tired unit, and which he doesn't attempt to solve.

The camp was the most unpleasant I ever remember, on a deep layer of fine dust, of a dark,
dirty colour. A high wind rose, and eyes, ears,
mouth, food, and kit, were soon full of it.
Roasting hot too. There was a long ride to
water, and then I got some sleep behind my
upturned saddle, waking with my eyes glued up.
To watering again and evening stables. The
wind went down about six and things were
better. None of us drivers had blankets, though,

for the kit-waggon had for some reason been
left at Pynaar's River.   However, I shared a bed
with another chap, and was all right.

August 24.—I am now cursing my luck in an
ambulance waggon.   For several days I have
had a nasty place coming on the sole of my
foot, a veldt-sore, as it is called.   To-day the
doctor said I must go off duty, and I was
told to ride on one of our transport-waggons.
This sounds simple ; but I knew better, and
made up my mind for some few migrations, before
I found a resting place.   With the help of
Williams I first put myself and my kit on one of
our waggons.   Then the Major came up, and was
very sympathetic, but said he was sending back
one waggon to Pynaar's River, and I had better
go on that, and not follow the Battery.   So I
migrated there and waited for the next move.
It came in a general order from the Staff that
nothing was to go back.   I was to seek an
asylum in an R.A.M.C. ambulance waggon.   So
we trudged over to an officer, who looked at my
foot and said it was all very well, but he had no

rations for me. However, rations were sent for, and I got into a covered waggon, with seats to hold about eight men, sat down with six others, Munsters and Wilts men, and am now waiting for the next move. It is 11 A.M. and we have not inspanned yet, though the battery and most of the brigade have started. I hear the whole column is to go to Warm Baths, sixteen miles farther on.

We didn't start till 1.30, and halted about five. They are very pleasant chaps in the waggon, and we had great yarns about our experiences. They were in a thorough "grousing" mood. To "grouse" is soldiers' slang for to "complain." They were down on their scanty rations, their hot brown water, miscalled coffee, their incessant marching, the futility of chasing De Wet, everything. Most soldiers out here are like that. To the men-calculators and battle-thinkers it doesn't matter very much, for Tommy is tough, patient, and plucky. He may "grouse," but he is dependable. It came out accidentally that they had been on half-rations

Q

of biscuit for the last two days, and that day
had had no meat issued to them, and only a
biscuit and a half. By a most lucky hap,
Williams and I had the night before bought a
leg of fresh pig from a Yeomanry chap, and had
it cooked by a nigger. In the morning, when
we separated, I had hastily hacked off a chunk
for him, and kept the rest, and we now had a
merry meal over the national animal of the
Munsters. It was pleasant to hear the rich
Cork brogue in the air. It seems impossible to
believe that these are the men whom Irish
patriots incite to mutiny. They are loyal, keen,
and simple soldiers, as proud of the flag as any
Britisher. At five we outspanned, with orders
to trek again at the uncomfortable hour of 1 A.M.
The Orderly-corporal left me and a Sergeant
Smith of the Munsters to sleep on the floor of
the waggon, and the rest slept in a tent. They
gave us tea, and later beef-tea. The sergeant
and I sat up till late, yarning. He is a married
reservist with two children, and is more than
sick of the war. They gave us three blankets

between us, and we lay on the cushions placed
on the floor, and used the rugs to cover us both.
After some months of mother earth this unusual
bed gave me a nightmare, and I woke the
sergeant to tell him that the mules were
trampling on us, which much amused him.
These worthy but tactless animals were tethered
to the waggon, and pulling and straining on it
all the time, which I suppose accounted for my
delusion.

August 25.—*Saturday.*—At 1 A.M. the rest
tumbled in on us, and we started off for the
most abominable jolt over the country. For a
wonder it was a very cold night, and of course
we were all sitting up, so there was no more
sleep to be got. At sunrise we arrived at Warm
Baths, which turns out to be really a health-
resort with hot springs. The chief feature in
this peculiar place is a long row of tin houses,
containing baths, I hear; also an hotel and a
'railway station, then the bush-covered veldt,
abrupt and limitless. Baden-Powell and his
troops are here, and I believe the Boers are

behind some low hills which lie north of us, and
run east and west.   Our cart halted by a stream
of water, which I washed in, and found quite
warm.   Coffee and biscuits were served out.   A
lovely day, hot, but still, so no dust.   The
column stops here a day or so, I hear.   We have
been transferred to a marquee tent, where fifteen
of us lie pretty close.   The Battery is quite
near, and Williams has been round bringing my
blankets, for it appears the drivers' kits have
come on from Pynaar's River.   Several fellows
came round to see me, and Williams brought
some duff, and Ramsey some light literature ;
Williams also brought a *Times*, in which I
read about the massacre in China.   I'm afraid
the polyglot avengers will quarrel among themselves.   Restless night.   I believe I shall never
sleep well under a roof again.   A roof in London
will be a bit smutty, though.

August 26.—Breakfast at seven.   Told we
were going to shift.   Packed up and shifted
camp about a mile to some trees ; the other site
was horribly smelly.   Installed again in a tent.

I have a hardened old shell-back of a Tommy
(Yorkshire Light Infantry) on my right, and a
very nice sergeant of the Wilts Regiment on
my left. Some of the former's yarns are very
entertaining, but too richly encrusted with words
not in the dictionary to reproduce. How
Kipling does it I can't think. The sergeant is a
fine type of the best sort of reservist. He aston-
ished me by telling me he had been a deserter,
long ago, when a lad, after two years in the
Rifle Brigade, where he was sickened by tyranny
of some sort. He confessed, after re enlistment, and was pardoned. He had been fourteen
years in his present corps, and had got on well.
Opposite is a young scamp of Roberts's Horse.
Looks eighteen, but calls it twenty-two: his
career being that he was put in the Navy, ran
away, was apprenticed to the merchant service,
ran away (so forfeiting the premium his
parents had paid), shipped to the Cape, and
joined Roberts's Horse. I asked him what he
would do next. "Go home," he said, "and do
nothing." If I were his father I'd kick him out.

He's a nice boy, though. There are several
Munsters, jolly chaps, and a Tasmanian of the
Bush contingent, tall, hollow-eyed, sallow-faced
fellow, with dysentery—a gentleman, and an
interesting one. Williams has been here a
good deal. He made some tea for the two of
us in the evening, and we talked till late. I
am on ordinary "camp diet," which means tea,
biscuit, and bully-beef or stew. They give us
tea at four, and nothing after, so one gets pretty
hungry. Some men are on milk diet.

August 27.—*Monday.*—My foot gets on very
slowly. Veldt-sores, as they are called, are very
common out here, as though you may be per-
fectly well, as I am, the absence of fresh food
makes any scratch fester. Most entertaining
talks with the other chaps in the tent. The
Captain has been several times, and brought
papers.

August 28.—This is a very free-and-easy
field hospital; no irksome regulations, and
restrictions, and inspections. A doctor comes
round in the morning and looks at each of us.

The dressings are done once in twenty-four
hours by an orderly. He is a very good chap,
but you have to keep a watchful eye on him,
and see that he doesn't put the same piece of
lint on twice; yet you must be very tactful in
suggestions, for an orderly is independent, and
has the whip-hand. An officer walks round
again in the evening, pretty late, and says he
supposes each of us feels better. This very
much amused me at first, but, after all, it
roughly hit off the truth. We are nearly all
slight cases. Meals come three times a day, and
otherwise we are left to ourselves. The food might,
I think, be better and more plentiful. I have
had the privilege of hearing Tommy's opinions
on R.A.M.C. orderlies, and also those of an
R.A.M.C. orderly on Tommy, or perhaps rather
on his own status and grievances in general.
Inside the tent Tommy was free and unequivocal
about the whole tribe of orderlies, the criticism
culminating in a ghoulish story from my
right-hand neighbour, told in broadest Yorkshire,
about one in Malta, " who stole the —— boots

off the —— corpse in the —— dead-'ouse."
Outside the tent a communicative orderly poured
into my ear the tale of Paardeberg, and its unspeakable horrors, the overwork and exhaustion
of a short-handed medical corps, the disease and
death in the corps itself, etc. I conclude that
in such times of stress the orderly has a very
bad time, but that with a column having few
casualties and little enteric, like this, he is uncommonly well off. His class has done some
splendid work, which Tommy sometimes forgets,
but it must be remembered that it had to be
suddenly and hurriedly recruited with untrained
men from many outside sources, some of them
not too suitable. My impression is that they
want more supervision by the officers. The
latter, in this hospital, are, when we see them,
very kind, and certainly show the utmost in-
dulgence in keeping off duty men who are not
feeling fit for work.

CHAPTER XI.

HOSPITAL.

August 29.—Suddenly told we were all to
go to Pretoria by train, railway being just open,
it seems. I am disgusted with the slowness of
my foot, and at being separated from the
Battery. It goes to-morrow back to Pynaar's
River, and then joins a flying column of some
sort.

August 30.—I write lying luxuriously on a
real spring-mattress bed, between real sheets,
having just had my fill of real bread and real
butter, besides every comfort, in a large marquee
tent, with a wooden floor, belonging to the
Imperial Yeomanry Hospital, Pretoria. I landed
in this haven at four o'clock this morning, after
a nightmare of a journey from Warm Baths. We
left there about 2.30 P.M. yesterday, after long

delays, and then a sudden rush. Williams came
over to say good-bye, and the Captain, Lieutenant
Bailey and Dr. Thorne; also other fellows with
letters, and four of our empty cartridges as
presents for officers of the Irish Hospital in
Pretoria. We were put into a truck already
full of miscellaneous baggage, and wedged
ourselves into crannies. It was rather a lively
scene, as the General was going down by the
same train, and also Baden-Powell on his way
home to England. The latter first had a farewell muster of his men, and we heard their cheers.
Then he came up to the officers' carriage with
the General. I had not seen him before, and
was chiefly struck by his walk, which had a sort
of boyish devil-may-care swing in it, while in
dress he looked like an ordinary trooper, a
homely-looking service jersey showing below his
tunic. As the train steamed out we passed his
troops, drawn up in three sides of a square facing
inwards, in their shirt-sleeves. They sent up
cheer after cheer, waving their hats to Baden-
Powell standing on the gangway. Then the

train glided past camps and piles of stores,
till the last little outpost with its wood fire
was past, and on into the lonely bush. It
was dark soon, and I lay on my back among
sacks, rifles, kit-bags, etc., looking at the stars,
and wondering how long this new move would
keep me from the front. We stopped many
times, and at Hamman's Kraal took aboard some
companies of infantry. At intervals down the
line we passed little posts of a few men, sentries
moving up and down, and a figure or two poring
over a pot on a fire. About midnight, after a
rather uneasy slumber, I woke in Pretoria. Raining. With the patient, sheep-like passivity that
the private soldier learns, we dragged ourselves
and our kit from place to place according to
successive orders. A friendly corporal carried
my kit-sack, and being very slow on my feet,
we finally got lost, and found ourselves sitting
forlornly on our belongings in the middle of an
empty, silent square outside the station (just
where we bivouacked a fortnight ago). However, the corporal made a reconnaissance, while

I smoked philosophical cigarettes. He found the rest in a house near by, and soon we were sitting on the floor of a room, in a dense crowd, drinking hot milk, and in our right minds; sick or wounded men of many regiments talking, sleeping, smoking, sighing, and all waiting passively. A benevolent little Scotch officer, with a shrewd, inscrutable face, and smoking endless cigarettes, moved quietly about, counting us reflectively, as though we were a valuable flock of sheep. We sat here till about 2.30 A.M., when several waggons drove up, into which we crowded, among a jumble of kit and things. We drove about three miles, and were turned out at last on a road-side, where lanterns and some red-shawled phantoms were glimmering about. We sat in rows for some time, while officers took our names, and sorted us into medical and surgical classes. Then a friendly orderly shouldered my kit and led me into this tent. Here I stripped off everything, packed all my kit in a bundle, washed, put on a clean suit of pyjamas, and at about 4 A.M. was lying in this

delicious bed, dead-beat, but blissfully comfortable. Oddly, I couldn't sleep, but lay in
a dreamy trance, smoking cigarettes, with a
beatific red-caped vision hovering about in the
half light. Dawn and the morning stir came, with
fat soft slices of fresh bread and butter and tea.
I have been reading and writing all day with
every comfort. The utter relaxation of mind and
limb is a strange sensation, after roughing it on
the veldt and being tied eternally to two horses.

There are twelve beds in this tent, and many
regiments are represented among the patients ;
there is an Imperial Light Horse man, who has
been in most of the big fights, a mercurial Argyll
and Sutherland Highlander, with a witty and
voluble tongue; men of the Wilts, Berks, and
Yorks regiments, and in the next bed a trooper
of the 18th Hussars, who was captured at Talana
Hill in the first fight of the war, had spent seven
months at Waterval in the barbed-wire cage
which we saw, and two since at the front. It
was under his bed that the escape-tunnel was
started. He gave me an enthusiastic account

of the one "crowded hour of glorious life" his squadron had had before they were captured. They got fairly home with the steel among a party of Boers in the hills at the back of Dundee, and had a grand time; but soon after found themselves surrounded, and after a desperate fight against heavy odds the survivors had to surrender.

September 2.—Getting very hot. Foot slow. The reaction has run its course, and I am getting bored.

September 4.—*Monday.*—In the evening got a cable from "London," apparently meant for Henry (my brother), saying "How are you?" and addressed to "Hospital, Pretoria." Is he really here, sick or wounded? Or is it a mistake for me, my name having been seen in a newspaper and mistaken for his? I have heard nothing from him lately, but gather that his corps, Strathcona's Horse, is having a good deal to do in the pursuit of Botha, Belfast way.

September 5.—Got the mounted orderly to try and find out about Henry from the other hospitals (there are many here), but, after saying he would, he has never turned up and can't be found. There are moments when one is exasperated by one's helplessness as a private soldier, dependent on the good-nature of an orderly for a thing like this.

September 6.—*Wednesday.*—A man came in yesterday who had been a prisoner of De Wet for seven weeks, having been released at Warm Baths the day I left. He said De Wet had left that force a week before, taking three hundred men, and had gone south for his latest raid. He thought that De Wet himself was a man of fair ability, but that the soul of all his daring enterprises was a foreigner named Theron. This man has a picked body of thirty skilled scouts, riding on picked horses, armed only with revolvers, and ranging seven or eight miles from the main body. De Wet always rode a white horse, and wore a covert coat. By his side rode ex-President Steyn, unarmed. The prisoners were fed as well as the Boers themselves, but that was badly, for they were nearly always

short of food, and generally had only Kaffir
corn, with occasional meat. One day a prisoner
asked a field-cornet when they were going to get
something to eat. " I don't care if you're a brass
band," he said, " but give us some food." " Well,
I'm very sorry," was the apologetic reply, " we've
been trying for a week to get one of your
convoys ; it will be all right when we get it."
De Wet himself was very pleasant to them, and
took good care they got their proper rations.
They rode always on waggons, and he spoke
feelingly of the horrible monotony of the jolt,
jolt, jolt, from morning to night. They nearly
always had a British force close on their heels,
and no sooner had they outspanned for a
rest than it would be " Inspan—trek." " Up
you get, Khakis ; the British are coming ! "
Then pom-pom-pom, whew-w-w-w, as shells
came singing over the rear-guard. At these
interesting moments they used to put the
prisoners in the extreme rear, so that the British
if they saw them, could not fire. He accounted for
the superior speed of the Boers by their skill in

managing their convoy; every Boer is a born driver (in fact, most of their black drivers had deserted), and they take waggons over ground we should shudder at, leaving the roads if need be, and surmounting impossible ascents. Again they confine their transport to the limits of strict necessity, and are not cumbered with all the waggon-loads of officers' kit which our generals choose to allow. Their rapidity in inspanning is marvellous; all the cattle may be scattered about grazing, but in five minutes from the word "Trek!" they are inspanned and ready. Their horses, he said, were wretched, and many rode donkeys; how they managed to get about so well he never could understand, but supposed the secret of their success was this body of well-mounted, reliable scouts, who saved all unnecessary travelling to the main body. A very large proportion of the Boer force were foreigners—French, Germans, Dutch, Russians, Norwegians.

The soul of this tent is Jock, an Argyll and Sutherland Highlander. He was wounded at

R

Modder River, and is now nominally suffering
from the old wound, but there is nothing really
the matter with him; and as soon as the Sister's
back is turned, he turns catherine wheels up the
ward on his hands. His great topic is the glory
and valour of the Highland Brigade, discoursing
on which he becomes in his enthusiasm unintel-
ligibly Scotch. It is the great amusement of
the rest of us to get rises out of him on the
subject, and furious arguments rage on the
merits of various regiments. He is as simple as
a child, and really seems to believe that the
Highland Brigade has won the war single-
handed. He is no hand at argument, and gets
crushing controversial defeats from the others,
especially some Berks men, but he always takes
refuge at last " in the thun rred line," as his
last entrenchment. "Had ye ever a thun rred
line?" he asks, and they quail. The matter
came to a crisis yesterday, when one of them
produced a handbook on British regiments
and their histories. The number of "honours"
owned by each regiment had been a hotly

contested point, and they now sat down and
counted them. The Royal Berks had so
many—Minden, Waterloo, Salamanca, Vittoria,
Sevastopol, etc. In breathless silence those
accredited to the Argyll and Sutherland Highlanders were counted. There were fewer, and
Jock was stunned at first. " Ah, but ye ha' not
counted the thun rred line," he shouted.
' Ga'rn, what battle's that ? " they scoffed.
" The battle of the thun rred line," he persisted.
Balaclava was on his list, but he didn't even
know it was there that his gallant regiment
formed the thin red line. Yet he had his
revenge, for, by a laborious calculation, lasting
several hours, it was found that the united
honours of the Scotch regiments were greater
than the united English or Irish.

September 6.—*Thursday.*—I am allowed to
go to a chair outside the tent, a long, luxurious
canvas lounge. In the valley below and to the
right lies Pretoria, half buried in trees, and
looking very pretty. Behind it rises a range of
hills, with a couple of forts on the sky-line.

Across the valley lies quite a town of tents,
mostly hospitals. We all of us live in pyjamas;
some wear also a long coat of bright blue.
Sisters flit about, dressed in light blue, with
white aprons and veils, and brilliant scarlet
capes, so that there is no lack of vivid colour.
A road runs in front of the tent; an occasional
orderly gallops past, or a carriage passes with
officers.

September 7.—To my delight this afternoon,
I heard a voice at my tent door, saying,
"Is Childers here?" It turned out to be
Bagenal, one of the released Irish Yeomanry, and
a friend of Henry's, who had come from him to
look for me. Henry is wounded in the foot, but
now "right as rain." He is in the Convalescent
Camp, which is plainly visible from here, about a
mile off. It seems that by another lucky coincidence he received letters meant for me, and so
knew I was in Pretoria. The whole affair abounds
in coincidences, for had I answered the cable home
I should have said "foot slight," or something
like it, and he would have said the same. It

would have done for either. We are lucky to
have found one another, for the Secretary's
inquiries led to nothing.

I have been reading in the *Bloemfontein Post*
a report of the Hospital Commission. I have
no experience of General Hospitals, but some of
the evidence brings out a point which is
heightened by contrast with a hospital like this,
and that is the importance of close supervision
of orderlies, on whom most of the comfort
of a patient depends. To take one instance
only ; if a man here is ordered port wine, it
is given him personally by the Sister. To
give orderlies control of wine and spirits is
tempting them most unfairly. On the whole,
I should say this hospital was pretty well
perfect. The Sisters are kindness itself. The
orderlies are well-trained, obliging, and strictly
supervised. The Civil Surgeon, Dr. Williams,
is both skilful and warm-hearted. There is
plenty of everything, and absolute cleanliness
and order.

The Strange Story of the Occupation and Surrender of Klerksdorp, as told by a Trooper of the Kimberley Light Horse, taken Prisoner about July 10, *by De Wet, released at Warm Baths on August* 28, *and now in this ward.*

Early in June, twenty-one men and four officers of the Kimberley Light Horse rode out thirty miles from Potchefstroom, and summoned the town of Klerksdorp to surrender. It is a town of fair size, predominantly Dutch, of course, but with a minority of English residents. The audacious demand of the Liliputian force was acceded to. They rode in, and the British flag was hoisted. With charming effrontery it was represented that the twenty-one were only the forerunners of an overwhelming force, and that resistance was useless. The Dutch were cowed or acquiescent, and a splendid reception was given to the army of occupation; cheering, flag-waving, and refreshments galore. Their commanding officer mounts the Town Hall steps, and addresses the townspeople, congratulating them on their

loyalty, announcing the speedy end of the war,
hinting at the hosts of British soon to be
expected, and praising the Mayor, a brother of
General Cronje, for his wise foresight in sub-
mitting ; in return for which he said he would
try to obtain the release of the General from
Lord Roberts. The troop is then escorted by a
frantic populace to their camping ground ;
willing hands off-saddle the horses, while others
ply the tired heroes with refreshments. The
town is in transports of joy. Days pass. The
news spreads, and burghers come in from all
sides to deliver up their arms to the Captain.
He soon has no fewer than twelve hundred rifles,
of which he makes a glorious bonfire, thus
disarming at one stroke a number of Boers
fifty times greater than his own force. There
is no sign of the overwhelming forces of the
British, but their early arrival is daily predicted,
and the delay explained away. Meanwhile, the
twenty-one live in clover, eating and drinking
the best of everything, and overwhelmed with
offers of marriage from adoring maidens. Luxury

threatens to sap their manhood. Guards and patrols are unsteady in their gait; vigilance slackens. A grand concert is given one night, during which the whole army of occupation is inside one room. Two guards are outside, but these are Dutch police. At this moment a handful of determined enemies could have ended the occupation, and re-hoisted the Boer flag. Weeks pass, still the British do not come, but the twenty-one hold sway, no doubt by virtue of the moral superiority of the dominant race.

But at last their whole edifice of empire tumbles into ruin with the same dramatic suddenness with which it rose. The ubiquitous De Wet marches up and surrounds the town with an overwhelming force; the inevitable surrender is made, and the Boer flag flies again over Klerksdorp after six glorious weeks of British rule by a score or so of audacious troopers.

September 8.—Henry turned up in a carriage and pair, and we spent all the afternoon together. It is a strange place to meet in after seventeen months, he coming from British Columbia, I from London. A fancy strikes me that it is symbolic of the way in which the whole empire has rallied together for a common end on African soil. He is still very lame, though called convalescent, and we are trying to work his transfer over here. The day-sister has very kindly written a letter to the commanding officer at his camp about it. We compared notes, and found we had enough money to luxuriously watch his carriage standing outside at five shillings an hour. It cost a pound, but it was worth it. We had so much to talk about, that we didn't know where to begin. A band was playing all the afternoon, and a tea-party going on somewhere, to which Miss Roberts came. She came round the tents also and talked to the men. It turns out that Henry and I both came down from the front on the same day from widely different places, for he was wounded at Belfast, under Buller.

September 9.—Jock gave us a complete concert last night, songs, interspersed with the

maddest, most whimsical patter, step-dances,
ventriloquism, recitations. He kept us in roars
for a long time. Blended with the simplicity of
a baby, he has the wisdom of the serpent, and
has the knack of getting hold of odd delicacies,
with which he regales the ward. He is per-
fectly well, by the way, but when the doctor
comes round he assumes a convincing air of
semi-convalescence, and refers darkly to his old
wound. The doctor is not in the least taken in,
but is indulgent, and not too curious. As soon
as his back is turned, Jock is executing a reel in
the middle of the ward.

The I.L.H. man is very interesting. Like
most of his corps, which was recruited from the
Rand, he has a position on a mine there, and
must be well over forty. He had been through
the Zulu war too. His squadron was with
Buller all through the terrible struggle from
Colenso to Ladysmith, which they were the first
to enter. They were shipped off to the Cape
and sent up to relieve Mafeking with Mahon.
He has been in scores of fights without a scratch,

but now has veldt sores. He says Colenso was by far the worst battle, and the last fortnight before the relief of Ladysmith was a terrible strain. But he spoke very highly of the way Buller fed his men. The harder work they did, the better they fared. (The converse is usually the case.) I have heard the same thing from other fellows; there seem to have been very good commissariat arrangements on that side of the country. From first to last all men who served under Buller seemed to have liked and trusted him. Curiously enough, he says that Ladysmith was in far worse case than Mafeking when relieved. The latter could have held out months longer, he thinks, and they all looked well. In Ladysmith you could have blown any of them over with a puff of air, and the defence was nearly broken down.

Judging from this casual intercourse, he represents a type very common among colonial volunteers, but not encouraged by our own military system—I mean that of the independent, intelligent, resourceful unit. If there are many

like him in his corps, it accounts amply for the
splendid work they have done. He told me that
not one of them had been taken prisoner, which,
looking at the history of the war, and at the kind
of work such a corps has to do, speaks volumes for
the standard of ability in all ranks. But what
I don't like, and can't altogether understand, is
the intense and implacable bitterness against the
Boers, which all South Africans such as him show.
Nothing is too bad for the Boers. " Boiling oil "
is far too good. Deportation to Ceylon is pitiful
leniency. Any suggestion that the civilized
customs of war should be kept up with such an
enemy, is scouted. Making all allowances for
the natural resentment of those who have known
what it is to be an Uitlander, allowing too for
" white flag " episodes and so on, I yet fail to
understand this excess of animosity, which goes
out of its way even to deny any ability to Boer
statesmen and soldiers, regardless of the slur
such a denial casts on British arms and states-
manship. After all, we have lost ten thousand
or more prisoners to the Boers, and, for my part,

the fact that I have never heard a complaint of
bad treatment (unnecessarily bad, I mean) from
an ex-prisoner, tells more strongly than anything
with me in forming a friendly impression of the
enemy we are fighting. Many a hot argument
have we had about Boer and Briton; and I'm
afraid he thinks me but a knock-kneed im-
perialist.

September 10. — *Monday.* — To my great
delight, Henry turned up as an inmate here, the
commanding officer at the convalescent camp
having most kindly managed his transference,
with some difficulty. The state of his foot didn't
enter into the question at all, but official " eti-
quette" was in danger of being outraged. The
commanding officer was a very good chap, though,
and Henry seems to have escaped somehow in the
tumult, unpursued. He had to walk over here.

A wounded man from Warm Baths came in
to-day, and said they had had two days' fighting
there ; camp heavily shelled by Grobelaar.

September 13.—*Thursday.*—Foot nearly well,
but am not allowed to walk, and very jealous of

Henry, who has been given a crutch, and makes rapid kangaroo-like progress with it. There are a good many in his case, and we think of getting up a cripples' race, which Henry would certainly win.

Letters from Williams and Ramsey at the front. It seems Warm Baths is evacuated, and the Brigade has returned to Waterval. Why? However, it's nearer here, and will give me a chance of rejoining earlier.

A splendid parcel arrived from home. A Jäger coat, chocolate, ginger, plums, cigarettes. Old Daddy opposite revels in the ginger; he is the father of the ward, being forty-seven, a pathetic, time-worn, veldt-worn old reservist, utterly done up by the fatigues of the campaign. He has had a bad operation, and suffers a lot, but he is always " first-rate, couldn't be more comfortable," when the Sisters or doctors ask him; " as long as I never cross that there veldt no more," he adds.

A locust-storm passed over the hospital to-day — a cloud of fluttering insects, with dull red bodies and khaki wings.

September 15.—*Saturday.*—My foot is well, at any rate for moderate use, and I am to go out on Monday. What I should like, would be to rejoin at once, but unfortunately one has first to go through the intermediate stages of the Convalescent camp, and the Rest camp, where " details " collect, to be forwarded to their regiments. I don't look forward to being a detail at all. Henry's foot is much better, and he is to go out on Monday too. He is still rather lame, though. It has been most delightful having him here.

.The evenings are deliciously cool, and you can sit outside in pyjamas till 8.30, when you are turned in. We sat out for long last night, talking over plans. A staff officer has twice been in here, and seemed much amused by us two brothers having fore-gathered. I asked him about Paget's brigade, and he seemed to think they were still at or near Waterval.

September 16.—*Sunday.*—We went to church in the evening; a tent pleasantly filled up, a

Sister at the harmonium, hymns, a few prayers, the Psalms, and a short sermon; a strange parti-coloured congregation we were, in pyjamas, slippers and blue coats, some on crutches; Sisters in their bright uniforms. Chairs were scarce, and Henry and I sat on the floor. It was dark before the end, and in the dim light of two candles at the harmonium we looked a motley throng.

Both bound for the Convalescent camp to-morrow.

September 17.—*Monday.*—What we actually did to-day, seeing the commandant, regaining our kit, drawing new kit, might have been done in half an hour; but we took from nine till three doing it, most of which time we were standing waiting. However, about three we found ourselves in a covered cart with five others and our kits, bound for the Convalescent camp. We had said good-bye to the Sisters and our mates. Old Daddy, I am glad to say, had "worked it," as they say, and was radiant, having been marked up for home.

No more of "that there veldt" for him. Jock
had already been sent out and given a post
as hospital orderly, and was now spreading the
fame of the Highland Brigade in new fields.
We both felt, on the whole, that we had
been looked after very well in a very good
hospital.

The mules jolted us across the valley, and
landed us at a big block of tents, and we took
places in one ; mother earth again. Tea, the
milkless variety again, at 4.30, and then we
went to Henry's old tent in the General Hospital,
which adjoins this camp, and talked to a friend
of his there, a man in the Rifle Brigade, with a
bad splintered knee. He was shot about the
same time as Henry in a fine charge made
by his battalion, which I remember reading
about.

Both much depressed to-night ; the atmosphere of this camp is like a convict settlement.
The food and arrangements are all right, but
nobody knows any one else ; all are casual details
from every possible regiment and volunteer corps

s.

in the Empire. Nearly all are " fed up ; " nearly all want to get home. A vein of bitter pessimism runs through all conversations ; there is a general air of languor and depression. Fatigues are the only occupation. I should go melancholy mad here, if I stayed ; but I shall apply to return to the Battery. Even then there is another stage —the Rest camp—to be gone through. We sat up late this night outside the lines, talking of this strange coincidence of our meeting, and trying to plan future ones. He feels the same about this place, but is still too lame to rejoin his corps.

September 18.—We washed in a stream some distance off, and then had breakfast. Then general parade. There must be some two or three hundred of us, and a wretched, slipshod lot we looked. A voice said, " Those who want to rejoin their regiments, two paces to the front." A few accepted the invitation. I gave in my name, and was told to parade again at two, with kit packed. The next moment we were being split up into fatigue parties. Fatigues are always a nuisance, but I don't mind them under my own folk, with a definite necessary job to be done. A fatigue under strange masters and with strange mates is very irksome, especially when, as in this case, there is little really to be done, but they don't want to leave you idle. This was a typical case. I and a dozen others slouched off under a corporal, who showed us to a sergeant, who gave us to a sergeant-major, who pointed to a line of tents (Langman's Hospital), and bade us clean up the lines. To the ordinary eye there was nothing to clean up, but to the trained eye there were some minute fragments of paper and cigarette ends. Now the great thing in a fatigue of this kind is : (1) To make it last. No good hurrying, as fresh futilities will be devised for you. (2) To appear to be doing something at all costs. (3) To escape unobtrusively at the first opportunity. There are some past-masters in the theory and practice of fatigues who will disregard No. 1, and carry on No. 2 till the golden moment when, with inspired audacity, they achieve No. 3, and vanish

from the scene. This requires genius. The less
confident ploddingly fulfil Nos. 1 and 2, and
don't attempt No. 3. Well, we loitered up and
down, and collected a few handfuls, and when
we had eked out the job to the uttermost, stood
together in a listless knot and waited. "What
shall we do?" we asked the corporal. "Do
any —— thing," he despairingly cried, "but do
some —— thing!" By this time the sergeant-
major too was at his wits' end as he looked
round his spotless lines. But you can't easily
baffle a sergeant-major. There was a pump,
with a big tub by it, to catch the waste, I
suppose. The artistic possibilities of these
simple objects flashed across him. In his mind's
eye he saw this prosaic tub sublimed into a
romantic pool, and girdled by a rockery, in whose
mossy crannies errant trickles of water might
lose themselves, and perhaps fertilize exotic
flora yet unborn. At this moment I espied a
wheelbarrow in the distance, and went for it
with that purposeful briskness, which may sometimes be used in fatigues of this sort to disguise

your real intentions. For it is of the greatest
importance in a fatigue to have an implement;
it is the outward symbol of labour; if observation
falls on you, you can wipe your brow and
lean on it; you can even use it for a few
minutes if necessary. Without some stage
property of this sort only a consummate actor
can seem to be busy. Well, I got to the barrow
just in time. There were two; a Grenadier
Guardsman got the other, and amid envious
looks we wheeled them off towards a heap of
rubble in the offing, "conveniently low." Then,
with a simultaneous sigh of relief, we mechani-
cally produced our pipes and tobacco, found
comfortable seats against the pile of rubble, and
had a good chat, lazily watching the genesis of
the naiad's grotto in the distance. When we had
had a good smoke, and fought our battles over
again, we got up and saw signs that the
fatigue was guttering out; so we put a few
stones in each of the barrows, and, well content,
journeyed back to the scene of operations, and
laid our stones round the base of the tub, more

because we knew nowhere else to lay them than for any other reason, for the sergeant-major had apparently forgotten his grandiose designs in other schemes, and had disappeared. The fatigue party was thinning. The corporal said what may be freely translated as "disappear quietly," and we made off to our camp, where I found Henry, who had doctor's leave to be excused fatigues, being lame.

CHAPTER XII.

A DETAIL.

September 18, *continued.*—At two we paraded again with our kits, and about a dozen of us marched off to the Rest camp, which is the next stage. Everything was very hurried, but Henry had just time to tell me that he was ordered to Bloemfontein, when I had to start. We said good-bye, and I don't suppose will meet again till London. The Rest camp was about four miles off, on the other side of Pretoria. Arrived very hot and dusty. Waited some time, and then was told that I must go to the Artillery Barracks, another two miles in quite a different direction. I might just as well have gone there direct. However, I was lucky enough to get a lift for my kit and myself most of the way, and landed

about 5.30 at a collection of big, red-brick
buildings outside the town, was handed from
person to person for some time, and finally
found a resting-place on the floor of a huge
bare room in a sort of ·a tin outbuilding,
where some 150 R.A. men of all batteries
were sitting or lying on their kit round the
walls and down the centre; like lost souls,
I pictured them, sitting round one of Dante's
purgatorial retreats. I felt exactly like going
to school again for the first time, though, of
course, I soon found them all very friendly. I
learned that there was no food to be got till
to-morrow, but I foraged about till I found a
sort of canteen-tent, where they sold buns, and,
having some tea of my own, got water boiled
over a friendly fire, and now feel happier; but
I fervently hope I shall get back to the Battery
soon. When I heard last from Williams, they
had returned to Waterval after some hard forced
marching.

September 19.—Loafed away last evening
somehow. A wan electric light half lit the room

after dark; the souls "twittered" like Homer's in dejected knots. "Fatigues all day, and a pass into town once a week," seem to be the prospect. Reveillé to-day at six. At parade, after breakfast, I was told off to act as an office orderly to Captain Davies, the Inspector of Ordnance, an all-day job, but otherwise with possibilities in it, I judged. Found the office, swept it out, and dusted and tidied things. Parlour-maid's work is nearly new to me (I have only cleaned windows before, in barracks at St. John's Wood), and I found myself trying to remember what I used to see Mary doing in the flat. I fancy my predecessor must have been a "slattern," for everything was thick with dust. I wish the Captain would leave his matches behind; there is not a match to be got in Pretoria now for the ordinary mortal. I'm afraid there are no perquisites in this situation. Also I wish he would get a waste-paper basket. I have made a humane resolve never to be without one myself, at home. Captain rode up about 9.30; I tied up his pony, and then

sat on a stone step outside, feeling rather like a
corner-boy trying to pick up a job. Found a
friendly collar-maker in a room near. He also is
a "detail," or "excess number," but a philosopher
withal. He told me that from his observation
I had a "soft job."—Nothing happened, so I
have adjourned to some tarpaulins in the back
yard. A shout of "Ord'ly" from the office
interrupted me, and I was sent with a blue
letter to the Chief Ordnance Officer in a camp
about a mile away. Again to the same place in
the afternoon, and one or two other little errands,
but between whiles I had plenty of time to
write. The Captain rode off about five, and I
somehow got attached to the collar-maker, who
was extremely friendly, and we spent the
evening together. Looked in at a S.C.A. tent,
and found a service going on. The Chaplain of
the Bushmen was speaking.

September 20.—I got a pass and walked to
Pretoria in the evening; saw the place by daylight, and was rather disillusioned. The good
buildings and the best shops are in a very small

compass, and are nothing much at the best, though the Palace of Justice and the Government buildings are tolerably dignified. All this part seems quite new. There is very little to be bought. Indeed, the wonder is that there is anything, for no trade supplies have come in since the war began. By way of testing prices, I took a cup of tea and some cake in a pleasant little shop; half a crown; worth it though, for the tea had fresh milk in it. Groceries seem unobtainable, but I made a valuable haul at a chemist's, in the shape of tea-tablets, which I think are the most useful things one can have out here. Matches can't be bought at all, but if you buy other things, and then are very polite, they will throw in a box for love; at least, a tobacconist did so for me. They used to be a shilling a box, but the authorities limited the price to a penny, a futile proceeding.

The charm of Pretoria lies in its outlying roads, with its cool little villas peeping out of green. The place is very quiet, and every one is in khaki.

September 21.—Can't get sent to the Battery

yet. Our tin room grows fuller. At night it is much too crowded, and is horribly stuffy; for the nights are very hot. But I am quite at home now, and enjoy the society, mixed though it is. I have literary arguments with a field-battery bombardier. We both rather pity one another, for he can't appreciate Thackeray and I can't understand Marie Corelli, whose works, with their deep spiritual meaning, he speaks of reverently. He hopes to educate me up to "Ardath," and I have offered him the reversion of "Esmond," which I bought yesterday.

Went down to town in the evening and visited the Irish Hospital, which has commandeered the Palace of Justice, and turned it to better uses than Kruger's venial judges ever put it to. The patients dwell " in marble halls," spacious, lofty rooms. Had a pleasant chat with Dr. Stoker. (The I. H. were shipmates of ours on the *Montfort.*) Also, to my great delight, found two men of our Battery there; it was a great treat to see familiar faces again. They said the Battery or part of it was at Waterval. I don't see why

I shouldn't rejoin at once if they will only let
me. I joined them in an excellent tea. They
spoke most highly of the hospital. I had no
pass to get back with, and didn't know the
countersign, but I bluffed through all right.

September 22.—No prospect of getting away,
though I apply daily to rejoin. Sent down to
Pretoria with a letter in the middle of the day,
so took the opportunity of visiting the Soldiers'
Home, where you can get mild drinks, read the
papers, and write. Visited the .Battery chaps
again in the evening. I have grown quite reck-
less about the lack of a pass ; " Orderly to Captain
Davies," said in a very off-hand tone I found an
excellent form of reply to sentries. I have an
" Esmond," and am enjoying it for about the
fiftieth time. It serves to pass away the late
evenings. A great amusement in the barrack-
room after dark is gambling. The amounts won
and lost rather astonish me. Happily it is done
in silence, with grim intensity. But I have only
an inch of candle, and can't buy any more. Next
me on the floor is a gunner of the 14th Battery,

which lost its guns at Colenso. He has just
given me a graphic account of that disastrous
day, and how they fought the guns till ammunition failed and then sat (what was left of them)
in a donga close behind, with no teams with
which to get more ammunition or retire the
guns. I have also had the story of Sanna's Post
from a U Battery man who was captured there.
He described how they were marching through
a drift one morning, with no thought of Boers
in their heads,. when they suddenly attacked at
close range, and were helpless. I may mention a
thing that strikes me about all such stories (and
one hears a good many out here) from soldiers
who have been "given away" by bad leader-
ship. There is criticism, jesting and satirical
generally, but very little bitterness. Bravery
is always admired, but it is so universal as to be
taken for granted. The popularity of officers
depends far more on the interest they show in
the daily welfare of the men, in personal good-
fellowship, in consideration for them in times of
privation and exhaustion, when a physical strain

which tells heavily on the man may tell lightly
on the officers. It is a big subject and a delicate
one, but rightly or wrongly, I have got the impression that more might be done in the army
to lower the rigid caste-barrier which separates
the ranks. No doubt it is inevitable and harmless at home, but in the bloody, toilsome business
of war it is apt to have bad results. Of course
is only part of the larger question of our general
military system, deep-rooted as that is in our
whole national life, and now placed, with all its
defects and advantages, in vivid contrast with an
almost exactly opposite system.

September 23.—*Sunday.*—Ammunition fatigue
for most of us, while I attended as office-boy as
usual, and was walking about with letters most
of the day. There are farriers and wheelers also
at work in this yard, so that one can always
light one's pipe or make a cup of tea at the
forge fire. Just outside are ranged a row of
antiquated Boer guns of obsolete types; I
expect they are the lot they used to show to
our diplomatic representative when he asked

vexatious questions about the "increasing arma-
ments." I believe the Boers also left quantities
of good stores here when Pretoria was abandoned. These are fine new barracks scarcely
finished. They enclose a big quadrangle. Three
or four batteries, horse and field, are quartered
in them now. Tried to get to Pretoria after
hours, but was stopped by a conscientious sentry,
who wanted my pass. I wished to get to the
station, with a vague idea of finding when there
would be a train to Waterval, and then running
away.

September 24.—Worried the Sergeant-Major
again, and was told that I might get away
to-morrow. Meanwhile, I am getting deeper
in the toils.

I was sitting on my tarpaulins writing, and
feeling rather grateful for the "softness" of
my job, when a shout of "Ord'ly!" sent me
into the office. The Captain, who is a good-
natured, pleasant chap, asked me if I could do
clerk's work. I said I was a clerk at home, and
thought I could. He said he thought I must

find it irksome and lonely to be sitting outside, and I might just as well pass the time
between errands in writing up ledgers inside.
I was soon being initiated into Ordnance
accounts, which are things of the most dia-
bolical complexity. Ordnance comprises practically everything; from a gun-carriage to a
nail; from a tent, a waggon, a binocular, a
blanket, a saddle, to an ounce of grease and all
the thousand constituents which go to make
up everything. These are tabulated in a book
which is a nightmare of subsections, and makes
you dizzy to peruse. But no human brain can
tabulate Ordnance exhaustively, so half the book
is blank columns, in which you for ever multiply
new subsections, new atoms of Ordnance which
nobody has thought of before. The task has a
certain morbid fascination about it, which I
believe would become a disease if you pursued
it long enough, and leave you an analytico-
maniac, or some such horror. Myriad bits of
ordnance are continually pouring in and pouring out, and the object is to track them, and

T

balance them, and pursue every elusive atom from start to finish. It may be expendible, like paint, or non-expendible, like an anvil. You feel despairingly that a pound of paint, born at Kimberley, and now at Mafeking, is disappearing somewhere and somehow; but you have to endow it with a fictitious immortality. An anvil you feel safer about, but then you have to use it somewhere, and account for its surplus, if there is any. Any one with a turn for metaphysics would be at home in Ordnance; Aristotle would have revelled in it.

It has just struck me that 1s. 5d. a day for a charwoman, a messenger and an accountant, to say nothing of a metaphysician, all rolled into one, is low pay. In London you would have to give such a being at least a pound a week.

September 25.—Ledgers, vouchers, errands, most of the day. Melting hot, with a hot wind. Good news from the Sergeant-major that he is putting in an application for a railway pass for me to Waterval, without waiting for the other formalities.

September 26.—*Wednesday.*—Hopes dashed to the ground. Commandant won't sign the application till some other officer does something or other, which there seems little chance of his doing.

CHAPTER XIII.

SOUTH AGAIN.

Ordered home—Back to the Battery—Good-bye to the horses —The charm of the veldt—Recent work of the Battery— Paget's farewell speech—Hard-won curios—The last bivouac —Roberts's farewell—The southward train—De Wet?— Mirages—A glimpse of Piquetberg road—The *Aurania*—Embarkation scenes—The last of Africa—A pleasant night.

SEPTEMBER 27 was a red-letter day. News came that all the C.I.V. were going home on the following Monday. I was overwhelmed with congratulations in the barrack-room. I exercised the Captain's Argentine in the afternoon, and visited the station, where I learnt that the Battery had been wired for, and had arrived, but was camped somewhere outside.

On the next day I got another charwoman-clerk appointed, said good-bye to my R.A. friends and the Captain, who congratulated

me too, and was free to find the Battery and
rejoin. After some difficulty, I found them
camped about four miles out, close to the C.I.V.
Infantry. It was delightful to walk into the
lines, and to see the old familiar scenes, and
horses, and faces. Every one looked more
weather-beaten and sunburnt, and the horses
very shaggy and hard-worked, but strong and
fit. My mare had lost flesh, but was still in
fine condition. The Argentine was lashing out
at the others in the same old way. Tiny, the
terrier, looked very weary and travel-stained
after much forced marching, which she had
loyally undergone to the last. Jacko had not
turned a hair.

Williams turned up with "Pussy" in a
lather, having been hunting for me all round
Pretoria. We ate bully-beef and biscuit together in the old style. I took my pair down
to water for the last time, "for auld lang
syne," and noticed that the mare's spine was
not the comfortable seat it used to be.

Then the last "boot and saddle" went, and

they were driven away with the guns and
waggons to the station, and thence to the
remount depôt, to be drafted later into new
batteries. Ninety-four horses were handed over,
out of a hundred and fourteen originally brought
from England, a most creditable record.

The camp looked very strange without the
horses, and it was odder still to have no watering or grooming to do. In the evening, the
change from barrack-room to veldt was most
delightful. We made a fire and cooked tea in
the old way, and talked and smoked under the
soft night sky and crescent moon. Then what
a comfortable bed afterwards! Pure air to
breathe, and plenty of room. I felt I had
hardly realized before how pleasant the veldt
life had been.

The Battery had done a great deal of hard work
since I left ; forced marches by night and day
between Warmbad, Pynaar's River, Waterval,
Hebron, Crocodile River, and Eland's River ;
generally with Paget, once under Colonel
Plumer, and once under Hickman. They had

shared in capturing several Boer laagers, and quantities of cattle. When they left the brigade, a commando under Erasmus was negotiating for a surrender, which was made a day or two later, as we afterwards heard. Altogether, they had done very good work, though not a round was fired. I only wish I could have been with them.

One thing I deeply regret missing, and that was Paget's farewell speech to us, when all agree that he spoke with real and deep feeling. One of our gunners took it down in shorthand, and here it is:—

" Major McMicking, Officers, non-commissioned officers, and men of the C.I.V. Battery,—

" Lord Roberts has decided to send you home, and I have come to say good-bye and to express my regret at having to part with you. We have been together now for some months, and have had rough times, but in its many engagements the C.I.V. Battery has always done its work well. Before my promotion I commanded a battalion, and I know what a heart-breaking it

is to lead gallant fellows up to a strong position
unsupported by artillery; and I made up my
mind that, if ever I had a separate command, I
would never advance infantry without an
artillery support. I was fortunate enough to
have your Battery with me, and it is very grati-
fying to know that everything we attempted has
been successful. Owing to the excellent practice
made by your guns, you have the satisfaction of
knowing that you have been the cause of great
saving of lives to the Infantry, and at times the
Cavalry. I am sorry to lose you, and I shall
miss you very much. There is more hard work
to be done; and you cannot realize what it is to
me to lose a body of men whom I knew I could
always rely upon. There are many episodes,
some of which will remain a lasting memory to
me. One in particular I might refer to, when,
two days after leaving Lindley, two companies of
Munster Fusiliers came unexpectedly under
heavy rifle-fire at short range; your guns coming
smartly into action, dispersed the enemy with a
few well-directed shrapnel. It was one of the

smartest pieces of work I have ever seen. On
another occasion, outside Bethlehem (I forget the
name of the place),* when in a rear-guard action
with De Wet, you advanced under a heavy
cross - fire of shrapnel, when you rendered
splendid service, and saved Roberts' Horse by
silencing two guns and smashing a third. On
that day not a single life was lost on our side.
On still another occasion, outside Bethlehem,
under heavy shell-fire from five guns in a strong
position, the steadiness with which your guns
were served would have done credit to the finest
troops in the Empire. There are other inci-
dents that I might mention, but these three
occur to me specially at the moment. You are
returning home to receive a hearty welcome,
which you undoubtedly deserve, and I hope you
will sometimes think of me, as I certainly shall
of you ; and now you can tell your friends what
I think of you. I wish you a safe and pleasant
voyage. Good-bye."

We shall also tell them what we thought of

* Bultfontein.

him. There was not a man of us but liked, admired, and trusted him—as I know did his whole brigade. And that he trusted us, is an honour we shall not forget.

It was good to be going home again ; but I think every one felt half sorry that we were not to share in finishing the work before his brigade. The whole C.I.V. regiment was being sent home together ; but the Infantry, of course, had done the bulk of their work when we began ours. It was curious that this was the first occasion on which the three arms of the C.I.V., Infantry, Mounted Infantry, and Artillery, had been united under one command.

We spent the next two days in preparations for departure, in sorting of harness, sifting and packing of kit, and great burnings of discarded rubbish.

On the first of October, Williams and I walked into Pretoria to do some business, and try and pick up some curios. We had an exhausting conflict with a crusty old Jew, with whom we bargained for scjamboks and knobkerries. It

was with great difficulty we got him to treat
with us at all, or even show us his wares. He
had been humbugged so often by khakis that
he would not believe we were serious customers,
and treated our advances with violence and
disdain. We had to be conciliatory, as we
wanted his wares, though we felt inclined to loot
his shop, and leave him for dead. After some
most extraordinary bargaining and after tempting
him with solid, visible gold, we each secured a
scjambok and a knobkerry at exorbitant prices,
and left him even then grumbling and growling.

Scjamboks are whips made of rhinoceros'
hide. They take a beautiful polish, and a good
one is indestructible. A knobkerry is a stick
with a heavy round knob for a head, overlaid,
head and stem, with copper and steel wire,
in ingenious spirals and patterns. The Kaffirs
make them.

, I also wired to my brother to meet our
train at Elandsfontein. He had written me,
saying he had been sent there from the Convalescent Camp, having the luck to find as his

commandant Major Paul Burn-Murdoch, of the
Royal Engineers, who was a mutual friend of
ours.

I was on picket duty that night—my last on
the veldt. The camp looked very strange with
only the four lines of men sleeping by their kits,
and a few officers' horses and a little knot of ten
mules for the last buck-waggon. It was an
utterly still moonlight night, only broken by
the distant chirruping of frogs and the occasional
tinkle of a mule's chain.

At seven the next morning we met the C.I.V.
Infantry and Mounted Infantry, and were all reviewed by Lord Roberts, who rode out with his
Staff to say good-bye to us. He made us a
speech we were proud to hear, referring particularly to the fine marching of the Infantry, and
adding that he hoped we would carry home to
the heart of the country a high opinion of the
regular British soldier, alongside whom we had
fought. That we certainly shall do. He pro-
phesied a warm reception at home, and said he
hoped when it was going on we would remember

one man, our Honorary Colonel, who would have
liked to be there to march at our head into the
city of London ; " good-bye and God speed."
Then we cheered him and marched away.

At half-past twelve we were at the station,
where the guns had already been entrained by a
fatigue party. Ours was the first of three trains,
and was to carry the Battery, and two companies
of Infantry. Williams and I secured a small
lair underneath a limber in an open truck, and
bundled in our kit. The platform was crowded
with officers and Tommies, and many and envious
were the farewells we had. Kilsby, of T Battery,
whom I had made friends with at the barracks,
was there to see me off. At 4.30, amidst great
cheering, we steamed out and began the thousand
mile run to Capetown, slowly climbing the long
wooded pass, under an angry, lowering sky. At
the top a stormy sun was setting in a glowing
furnace of rose-red. We hastily rigged some
tarpaulins over our limber, and escaped a wetting
from a heavy shower. We had managed to dis-
tribute and compress our kit so as to leave room

to lie down in, and after dark we lit a lantern
and played picquet. About eight we came to
Elandsfontein, and there on the platform were
my brother and Major Burn-Murdoch. The latter
hurried us off to the restaurant—forbidden ground
to us men as a rule, sat us down among the officers,
and gave us a rattling good dinner, while our comrades munched their biscuits outside. De Wet,
we heard, was ahead, having crossed the line with
1000 men, two nights ago, further south. We
agreed that it would be a happy irony if he
held up our train, the first to carry troops
homeward—the herald of peace, in fact; and
just the sort of enterprise that would tickle his
fancy. Suddenly the train jerked off, and I
jumped into my lair and left them. It was a
warm night, and we sat under the stars on the
seats of the limber, enjoying the motion and the
cool air. About ten we pulled up at a station,
and just after we had stopped, four rifle-shots
rapped out in quick succession not far ahead.
De Wet, we at once conjectured. In the darkness on our left we heard an impatient corporal

turning out his sleepy guard, and a stir and
clatter of arms. One of our companies of
infantry was also turned out, and a party formed
to patrol the line, outposts having reported
some Boers tampering with the rails. The
rest of the train was sound asleep, but we,
being awake, got leave to go with the patrol.
Williams borrowed a rifle from somewhere, but
I could not find a weapon. They made us
connecting files between the advance party and
main body, and we tramped up the line and over
the veldt for about an hour, but nothing happened,
and we came back and turned in.

De Wet let us alone, and for five days we
travelled peaceably through the well-known
places, sometimes in the pure, clear air of true
African weather, but further south through
storms of cold rain, when Scotch mists shrouded
everything, and we lay in the bottom of our
truck, on carefully constructed islands of kit
and blankets, among pools of water, passing
the time with books and cards. Signs of war
had not disappeared, and at every station down

to Bloemfontein were the same vigilant camps
(often with parties posted in trenches), more
charred remains of trains, and ever-present
rumours of raiding commandos.

One novel sight I saw in the interminable
monotony of desert veldt. For a whole afternoon there were mirages all along the horizon,
a chain of enchanted lakes on either side, on
which you could imagine piers, and boats, and
wooded islands.

At Beaufort West we dropped our "boys,"
the Kaffir mule-drivers; they left us in a great
hubbub of laughing and shouting, with visions
before them, I expect, of a golden age, based on
their accumulated wealth of high pay. We
passed Piquetberg Road about midnight of
October 6th. Plumbley, the store-keeper, was
there, and the belle of the village was holding a
moonlight levée at the end of the train. There
was a temporary clear from the rain here, but it
soon thickened down again. When we steamed
away I climbed out on the buffers (the only way
of getting a view), and had a last look at the

valley, which our wheels had scored in so many
directions. Tulbagh Pass, Bushman's Rock, and
the hills behind it were looking ghostly through
a humid, luminous mist; but my posture was not
conducive to sentimentality, as any one who tries
it will agree; so I climbed back to my island,
and read myself to sleep by a candle, while we
clattered and jolted on into the night.

When I woke at dawn on October 7th we were
standing in a siding at the Capetown docks, the
rain coming down in torrents, and Table Mountain
blotted out in clouds. Collecting our kit from
sopping crannies and corners, we packed it and
paraded at six, and marched off to the quay,
where the *Aurania*, our homeward transport,
lay. Here we gave in revolvers, carbines,
blankets, etc., were split up into messes, and,
after much waiting, filed off into the fore part
of the ship, descended a noisome-smelling funnel
by an iron staircase, and found ourselves on the
troop-deck, very similar to that of the *Montfort*,
only likely to be much more crowded; the same
low ceiling, with cross-rafters for kit and hooks

U

for hammocks, and close-packed tables on either side.

More C.I.V. had arrived, and the quays were swarming with soldiers and civilians. Williams had decided to stay and see something of Capetown, and was now to get his discharge. There were a few others doing so also. He was discharged in form, and drove away to the Mount Nelson Hotel, returning later disguised as a civilian, in a long mackintosh (over his uniform), a scarf, and a villainous-looking cap; looking, as he said, like a seedy Johannesburg refugee. But he was free! The Manager of his hotel, which, I believe, is the smartest in South Africa, had looked askance at his luggage, which consisted of an oat-sack, bulging with things, and a disreputable-looking bundle.

At about three there was a great shouting and heaving of the crowd, and the High Commissioner came on the scene, and walked down the quay through a guard of honour which we and the Infantry had contributed to form, industriously

kinematographed on his progress by a fat Jew.
Several staff-officers were with Milner, and a
grey-bearded gentleman, whom we guessed to
be Sir Gordon Sprigg. Milner, I heard, made
a speech somewhere. Then a band was playing,
and we were allowed half an hour off the ship.
Williams and I had our last talk on the quay,
in a surging crowd of khaki and civilian grey,
mingled with the bright hats and dresses of
ladies. Then bells began to ring, the siren to
bellow mournfully, and the band to play vale-
dictory tunes ("Say *Au revoir* and not Good-
bye," I thought rather an ominous pleasantry).
We two said good-bye, and I squeezed myself
up the gangway. Every inch of standing room
aboard was already packed, but I got a
commanding position by clambering high up,
with some others, on to a derrick-boom. The
pilot appeared on the bridge, shore-ropes were
cast off, "Auld Lang Syne" was played, then
"God save the Queen." Every hat on board
and ashore was waving, and every voice cheering,
and so we backed off, and steamed out of the basin.

Sober facts had now to be considered. There were signs of a heavy swell outside, and something about " the lift of the great Cape combers " came into my head. We all jostled down to tea, and made the best of our time. There was no mistake about the swell, and a terrific rolling soon began, which first caused unnatural merriment, and then havoc. I escaped from the inferno below, and found a pandemonium on deck. The limited space allotted to the troops was crammed, and at every roll figures were propelled to and fro like high-velocity projectiles. Shell-fire was nothing to it for danger. I got hold of something and smoked, while darkness came on with rain, and the horrors intensified. I bolted down the pit to get some blankets. One glance around was enough, and having seized the blankets, up I came again. Where to make a bed ? Every yard, sheltered and unsheltered, seemed to be carpeted with human figures. Amidships, on either side of the ship, there was a covered gallery, running beneath the saloon deck (a palatial empty space, with a few officers strolling about it). In the gallery on the weather side there was not an inch of lying room, though at every roll the water lapped softly up to and round the prostrate, indifferent bodies. On the lee side, which was dry, they seemed to be lying two deep. At last, on the open space of the main deck aft, I found one narrow strip of wet, but empty space, laid my blankets down, earnestly wishing it was the dusty veldt, and was soon asleep. It was raining, but, like the rest, misery made me indifferent. *Montfort* experience ought to have reminded me that the decks are always washed by the night watch. I was reminded of this about 2 A.M. by an un-sympathetic seaman, who was pointing the nozzle of a hose threateningly at me. The awakened crowd was drifting away, goodness knows where, trailing their wet blankets. I happened to be near the ladder leading to the sacred precincts of the saloon deck. Its clean, empty, sheltered spaces were irresistibly tempting, and I lawlessly mounted the ladder with my bed, lay down, and went to sleep again.

CHAPTER XIV.

CONCLUSION.

Impressions of the voyage—Sentry-go—Troopship—Limitations—
Retrospect—St. Vincent—Forecasts—The Start—The Needles
—Southampton Water—Landing—Paddington—A dream.

I AM not going to describe the voyage in detail.
Africa, with all it meant, was behind us, England
was before, and the intervening time, monotonous though it was, passed quickly with that
absorbing thought.   My chief impression is that
of living in an eternal jostle ; forming interminable *queues* outside canteens, washing-places,
and stuffy hammock-rooms in narrow alleys, and
of leisure hours spent on deck among a human
carpet of khaki, playing euchre, or reading the
advertisement columns of ancient halfpenny
papers. There was physical exercise, and a parade

every day, but the chief duty was that of
sentry-go, which recurred to each of us every
five days, and lasted for twenty-four hours.
The ship teemed with sentries. To look out
for fire was our principal function, and a very
important one it was, but I have also vivid
recollections of lonely vigils over water-tight
doors in stifling little alley-ways, of directing
streams of traffic up troop-deck ladders, and of
drowsy sinecures, in the midnight hours, over
deserted water-taps and empty wash-houses.
These latter, which contained fourteen basins
between fourteen hundred men, are a good
illustration of the struggle for life in those days.
That a sentry should guard them at night was
not unreasonable on the face of it, since I calculated that if every man was to appear washed
at the ten o'clock parade, the first would have
had to begin washing about six o'clock the night
before, allowing ten minutes for a toilet, but
unfortunately for this theory, the basins were
always locked up at night. Another grim
pleasantry was an order that all should appear

shaved at the morning parade. Luckily this
cynical regulation was leniently interpreted, for
the spectacle of fourteen hundred razors flashing
together in those narrow limits of time and space
was a prospect no humane person could view
with anything but horror.

There was plenty of time to reflect over our
experiences in the last nine months. Summing
mine up, I found, and thinking over it at home
find still, little but good in the retrospect.
Physically and mentally, I, like many others,
have found this short excursion into strict
military life of enormous value. To those who
have been lucky enough to escape sickness, the
combination of open air and hard work will act
as a lasting tonic against the less healthy conditions of town-life. It is something, bred up as
we have been in a complex civilization, to have
reduced living to its simplest terms and to have
realized how little one really wants. It is much
to have learnt the discipline, self-restraint, en-
durance and patience which soldiering demands.
(For a driver, it is a liberal education in itself

to have lived with and for two horses day and night for eight months !) Perhaps the best of all is to have given up newspaper reading for a time and have stepped one's self into the region of open-air facts where history is made and the empire is moulded; to have met and mixed with on that ground, where all classes are fused, not only men of our blood from every quarter of the globe, but men of our own regular army who had fought that desperate struggle in the early stages of the war before we were thought of; to have lived their life, heard their grievances, sympathized with their needs, and admired their splendid qualities.

As to the Battery, it is not for a driver in the ranks to generalize on its work. But this one can say, that after a long and trying probation on the line of communications we did at length do a good deal of work and earn the confidence of our Brigadier. We have been fortunate enough to lose no lives through wounds and only one from sickness, a fact which speaks highly for our hand-ling in the field by our officers, and for their

general management of the Battery. Incidentally,
we can fairly claim to have proved, or helped to
prove, that Volunteer Artillery can be of use in
war ; though how much skill and labour is involved in its sudden mobilization only the few
able men who organized ours in January last
can know.

To return to the *Aurania*.

On the 19th of October we were anchored
at St. Vincent, with the fruit-laden bum-boats
swarming alongside, and the donkey-engines
chattering, derricks clacking, and coal-dust
pervading everything.

Here we read laconic telegrams from London,
speaking of a great reception before us on
Saturday the 27th, and thenceforward the talk
was all of runs, and qualities of coal, and technical
mysteries of the toiling engines, which were
straining to bring us home by Friday night.
Every steward, stoker, and cabin boy had his
circle of disciples, who quoted and betted on
his predictions as though they were the utter-
ings of an oracle ; but the pessimists gradually

prevailed, for we met bad weather and heavy head-seas on entering the bay. It was not till sunrise on Friday itself that we sighted land, a white spur of cliff, with a faint suggestion of that long unseen colour, green, behind it, seen across some miles of wind-whipped foaming blue. The optimists said it was the Needles, the pessimists the Start; the latter were right, and we guessed we should have to wait till Monday before landing; but that did not lessen the delight of watching the familiar shores slide by till the Needles were reached, and then of feasting our eyes, long accustomed to the parched plains of Africa, on fields and hedges, and familiar signs of homely, peaceful life.

It was four o'clock when we dropped anchor in Southampton Water, and were shouting a thousand questions at the occupants of a tug which lay alongside, and learnt with wonder, emotion, and a strange sense of unworthiness, of the magnificent welcome that London had prepared for us.

The interminable day of waiting; the landing

on the quay, with its cheering crowds; that
wonderful journey to London, with its growing
tumult of feelings, as station after station, with
their ribboned and shouting throngs, flashed by ;
the meeting at Paddington with our comrades of
the Honourable Artillery Company, bringing us
their guns and horses; the mounting of a glossy,
smartly-equipped steed, which made me laugh-
ingly recall my shaggy old pair, with their dusty,
travel-worn harness ; all this I see clearly enough.
The rest seems a dream ; a dream of miles of
upturned faces, of dancing colours, of roaring
voices, of a sudden dim hush in the great Cathe-
dral, of more miles of faces under gaslight, of a
voice in a packed hall saying, " London is proud
of her ——," of disconnected confidences with
policemen, work-people, street-arabs, and finally
of the entry once more through the old grey gateway of the Armoury House. I expect the feelings
of all of us were much the same ; some honest
pride in having helped to earn such a welcome ; a
sort of stunned bewilderment at its touching and
passionate intensity ; a deep wave of affection

for our countrymen; and a thought in the background all the time of a dusty khaki figure still plodding the distant veldt—our friend and comrade, Atkins, who has done more and bloodier work than we, and who is not at the end of it yet.

THE END.

PRINTED BY WILLIAM CLOWES AND SONS, LIMITED, LONDON AND BECCLES.

Also published in facsimile in *The Spellmount Library of Military History* and available from all good bookshops. In case of difficulty, please contact Spellmount Publishers (Tel: 01580 893730).

HAMILTON'S CAMPAIGN WITH MOORE AND WELLINGTON during the Peninsular War by Sergeant Anthony Hamilton
Introduction by James Colquhoun
Anthony Hamilton served as a Sergeant in the 43rd Regiment of Foot, later the Oxford and Buckingham Light Infantry. He fought at Vimiero and took part in the retreat to Corunna, vividly describing the appalling conditions and the breakdown of the morale of the British Army. He subsequently fought at Talavera, Busaco, the Coa, Sabugal, Fuentes de Oñoro, Salamanca and Vittoria. He also volunteered to take part in the storming parties of the sieges of Ciudad Rodrigo and Badajoz. During these actions, he was wounded three times.

THE MILITARY ADVENTURES OF CHARLES O'NEIL by Charles O'Neil
Introduction by Bernard Cornwell
First published in 1851, these are the memoirs of an Irish soldier who served with Wellington's Army during the Peninsular War and the continental campaigns from 1811 to 1815. Almost unknown in the UK, as the author emigrated to America straight after, it includes his eye-witness accounts of the bloody battle of Barossa, the memorable siege of Badajoz – and a graphic description of the Battle of Waterloo where he was badly wounded.

ROUGH NOTES OF SEVEN CAMPAIGNS: in Portugal, Spain, France and America during the Years 1809–1815 by John Spencer Cooper
Introduction by Ian Fletcher
Originally published in 1869, this is one of the most sought-after volumes of Peninsular War reminiscences. A vivid account of the greatest battles and sieges of the war including Talavera, Busaco, Albuera, Ciudad Rodrigo, Badajoz, Vittoria, the Pyrenees, Orthes and Toulouse and the New Orleans campaign of 1815.

THE JOURNAL OF AN ARMY SURGEON DURING THE PENINSULAR WAR by Charles Boutflower
Introduction by Dr Christopher Ticehurst
A facsimile edition of a rare journal written by an army surgeon who joined the 40th Regiment in Malta in 1801 and subsequently served with it in the West Indies, South America and the Peninsular War. Described by his family 'as a man of great activity and a general favourite with all his acquaintances', he saw action from 1810 to 1813 including Busaco, Ciudad Rodrigo, Badajoz and Salamanca – gaining a well-deserved promotion to Surgeon to the staff of Sir Rowland Hill's Brigade in 1812.